# IMPLEMENTING THE FOUR LEVELS

## A PRACTICAL GUIDE FOR EFFECTIVE EVALUATION OF TRAINING PROGRAMS

### DONALD L. KIRKPATRICK

### JAMES D. KIRKPATRICK

BK

BERRETT–KOEHLER PUBLISHERS, INC.
San Francisco

Berrett-Koehler Publishers, Inc.
235 Montgomery Street, Suite 650
San Francisco, CA 94104-2916
Tel: (415) 288-0260; Fax: (415) 362-2512; www.bkconnection.com

**Ordering Information**

**Quantity sales.** Special discounts are available on quantity purchases by corporations, associations, and others. For details, contact the "Special Sales Department" at the Berrett-Koehler address above.

**Individual sales.** Berrett-Koehler publications are available through most bookstores. They can also be ordered directly from Berrett-Koehler: Tel: (800) 929-2929; Fax: (802) 864-7626; www.bkconnection.com.

**Orders for college textbook/course adoption use.** Please contact Berrett-Koehler: Tel: (800) 929-2929; Fax: (802) 864-7626.

**Orders by U.S. trade bookstores and wholesalers.** Please contact Ingram Publisher Services: Tel: (800) 509-4887; Fax: (800) 838-1149; E-mail: customer.service@ingrampublisherservices.com; or visit www.ingrampublisherservices.com/Ordering for details about electronic ordering.

Berrett-Koehler and the BK logo are registered trademarks of Berrett-Koehler Publishers, Inc.

Printed in the United Sates of America

Berrett-Koehler books are printed on long-lasting acid-free paper. When it is available, we choose paper that has been manufactured by environmentally responsible processes. These may include using trees grown in sustainable forests, incorporating recycled paper, minimizing chlorine in bleaching, or recycling the energy produced at the paper mill.

**Library of Congress Cataloging-in Publication Data**

Kirkpatrick, Donald L.
    Implementing the four levels : a practical guide for effective evaluation of training programs / Donald L. Kirkpatrick and James D. Kirkpatrick. —1st ed.
        p. cm.
    Includes bibliographical references and index.
    ISBN 978-1-57675-454-2 (pbk. : alk. paper)
    1. Employees—Training of—Evaluation.   I. Kirkpatrick, James D., 1952–
II. Title.
    HF5549.5.T7K5695 2007
    658.3'12404—dc22                                        2007025384

First Edition
12  11  10                    10  9  8  7  6  5  4  3

# Contents

*v*

# Foreword

Don and Jim Kirkpatrick's *Implementing the Four Levels* will undoubtedly prove to be a cherished and well-used tool throughout the learning and development (L&D) community. The beauty of this edition is that trainers, designers, training managers, and training executives will all benefit from its action-oriented design and approach to Don's timeless measurement principles.

Trainers will use the tools and case study discussions to shift their daily focus beyond the learner's reaction to having a strategic business impact via learning. Training managers will use the real-life examples and guidelines to prepare results-driven programs and training teams prior to opening a classroom for learning. Training executives will especially benefit from the "Building a Chain of Evidence" chapter (Chapter 7) as they look to quantify the business benefits of L&D organizations.

The design community will perhaps enjoy this edition greater than any other. Using actual business cases that illustrate Don's levels in reverse order, designers can see how interviewing key stakeholders and subject matter experts guarantees a design that directly links coursework to the needs of the organization.

As Albert Einstein was to the scientific community, Don Kirkpatrick is to the learning and development community. However, the difference is that in this edition, Don and Jim have found a way to make theory and principle simple and easily implemented regardless of the reader's L&D experience.

I have used Don and Jim's collective works to create training programs, training teams, and training organizations that are viewed by the business as a competitive advantage rather than a required expense. If you are looking for the silver bullet to take your L&D efforts from expense to cherished asset, you've found it in this terrific resource!

Jim Hashman
*Division Director*
*Sales Learning and Development*
*Comcast University*
*Southfield, Michigan*

# Foreword

In the world of training in business, industry, and government, theories and models are used to help design, develop, implement, and evaluate training. Their value is directly related to how well these tools help evaluate programs and achieve results such as improved morale, reduced turnover, improved customer satisfaction, increased sales, and increased profits. One of the biggest challenges training professionals have is to take these theories and models and apply them to their own organization.

Don's book, *Evaluating Training Programs: The Four Levels*, has been the standard for decades in helping training professionals develop and evaluate training programs. In his book, he provides a clear overview of each of the four levels, guidelines for each level, and case studies that highlight specific applications of the four levels in real-world situations. These case studies are written by folks in business, industry, education, and government and describe how Kirkpatrick's models were implemented and the results achieved.

There are three unique features of this new book:

- The active involvement of managers in the four-level process
- The numerous "best practice" examples for evaluating each level organized by chapter
- The building of a compelling "chain of evidence" to demonstrate the value of training to the business

Knowing the four levels is not enough. It is one thing to know what the four different levels are—it is an entirely different thing to work with managers and others to implement them. In this new book, Jim and Don take the next logical step and provide the reader with practical information on applying the model more effectively. Specifically, they present valuable help on making evaluation decisions and getting buy-in and support from management. In addition, they have reviewed each case study from the basic book and gleaned out the practical applications from them for the reader in an organized, comprehensive manner.

This book is complementary to *Evaluating Training Programs: The Four Levels.* It is not meant to replace it. I am delighted that you will not have to discover the practical ways to evaluate and improve training programs. You now have a resource that can help you be more effective in your role in implementing Kirkpatrick's four levels.

Dan Schuch
*Training Developer*
*PacifiCorp*
*Portland, Oregon*

# Preface

The purpose of this book is to make it easy for you, the reader, to understand the four levels that I (Don) have developed, and to obtain practical help on how to apply any one or all of them. The book is intended as an addition to and not a replacement for the basic book, *Evaluating Training Programs: The Four Levels*, third edition.

We have added three chapters and taken the forms, examples, and approaches from the basic book and inserted them into the appropriate chapters. For example, Chapter 3, "Evaluating Level 1: Reaction," contains select reaction forms and approaches from the case studies in the basic book.

The first chapter suggests how you can decide what to evaluate and at what levels. The answer, of course, is by analyzing the available resources.

The second chapter tells you why and how to get managers on board. They can be very helpful in developing curriculum and are needed to provide support and accountability when trainees move from the classroom to the job. Also, you will need their help when you evaluate levels 3 and 4, where you have no authority, only influence. Chapters 3–6 provide guidelines and practical help for evaluating at each of the four levels.

Finally, the last chapter, "Building a Chain of Evidence," explains why it is necessary to evaluate all the levels in *sequence* and not try to measure results without first evaluating at the first three levels. This is the best way to demonstrate the value of training.

We want to thank each of the following authors who contributed examples from their case studies that were an important part of the basic book: Derrick Allman, Jennifer Altzner, Merrill Anderson, Chris Arvin, James Baker, David Barron, Judy Brooke, Holly Burkett, Nuria Duran, Gena Gongora, Steven Jablonski, Abram Kaplan, Don Kraft, Gusti Lowenberg, Jordan Mora, Patrick O'Hara, Gillian Poe, Laura Rech, Dan Schuch, and Juan Pablo Ventosa. We also want to thank Sara Jane Hope, Chris Lee, and Beverly Scherf, who spent many hours reviewing an early draft from a reader's standpoint and offering helpful suggestions on how to improve it.

We are also grateful to Jeevan Sivasubramanian, Steve Piersanti of Berrett-Koehler, and especially the editors, Debbie Masi and Cheryl Adams, who transformed our contributions into the finished book.

We cannot forget Fern, my wife and Jim's mother, for her understanding, patience, and encouragement for all the hours we spent writing and rewriting the book.

If you have questions about what we offer in the way of programs, services, books, and inventories, please see our contact information in The Authors section.

Best wishes for finding this book of practical help in evaluating your programs.

Don and Jim

# IMPLEMENTING
# THE FOUR LEVELS

# Chapter 1

## Analyzing Your Resources

As the preface stated, this is a practical guide to help you understand and implement the "four levels" that I (Don) have developed for evaluating training programs. You have probably heard of them and perhaps implemented one or more of them. Before describing the specifics of implementing Reaction, Learning, Behavior, and Results, there are two introductory chapters that are critical to set the table for training and evaluation success. The first is "Analyzing Your Resources," and the second is "Getting Your Managers on Board."

In this chapter, we will describe an approach for analyzing your resources to determine

what programs to evaluate
at which of the four levels

The answer, of course, depends largely on the resources you have for evaluating. In most organizations, trainers wear many "hats," of which evaluation is one. A few organizations have specialists whose only job is to evaluate. The available resources in terms of people, time, and budget are the critical factors to consider when approaching these two issues.

Look first within the training function for any full-time professionals who can spend full time on evaluation. Then look at other training professionals who have evaluation as one of their responsibilities. Determine how much of their time can be devoted to evaluation. Unfortunately, many training department managers view evaluation as "a smile sheet, a pre- and postknowledge, and hope for the best." They do not understand the tremendous power of evaluation not only to improve courses and programs, but also to reinforce mission-critical behaviors on the job, and to demonstrate the value of their efforts. This often causes them to be reluctant to "release" resources dedicated to evaluation.

Second, look at related departments such as Human Resources. Are there people there who are ready, willing, and able to help in the evaluation process? How much time can they invest?

The third source of help is the line managers. If you have programs for salespeople, for example, how much help can you get from sales managers and others in the sales departments? If your programs are aimed at computer specialists, how much help can you get from Information Technology people? If you are teaching courses for supervisors, how much help can you get from their managers?

The final source of help can be outside consultants. Here, you look at your budget and see what you can afford.

When you add all of this help together, you can estimate how much time and effort you can give to evaluation. With the likelihood of limited training department resources, competing priorities that limit the help from other internal departments, questionable help from managers, and a limited budget for outside consultants, evaluation needs to be targeted to programs that will accomplish the best results.

As a case in point, a new program on leadership that was developed to leverage all other training and is a high-profile program in the eyes of executives should receive a full-blown, four-level effort, with the focus on demonstrating the value of the program to organizational goals. Another significant consideration is which programs executives are most interested in. For example, top executives may be most interested in programs on a "culture of service" when training managers are more interested in evaluating programs on "coaching." You may have a "selling job" if you can't do both and decide on the latter. Other considerations are which programs are going to be repeated, which programs are the most expensive, and which programs are the most likely to contribute significant bottom-line results. These factors will help you to determine what programs to evaluate, how robust your evaluation efforts should be, and which of the four levels you should emphasize.

We also strongly suggest that you take the right steps to ensure that training is actually accomplishing what it was intended to do and contributing to the bottom line. Don't think about evaluation in terms of demonstrating overall value until you are sure you have done all you can to ensure that your training programs are effective. If you evaluate and find that the training programs have not been effective, you will need to back up through levels 3, 2, and 1 and find the "snags"—the factors that are keeping maximization of learning from happening.

The second part of this chapter has to do with a simple statement—you want to do what you can to ensure that the program you have decided to deploy your resources to is one that is of the best quality possible. In other words, you want to do what you can to see that the program meets the needs of your stakeholders, the business problem or need, and is delivered in the most effective way possible for the group for which it is intended.

We have made a list of ten requirements for an effective training program. Actually, there are only nine, and the tenth one is evaluation. So, take care of the following requirements for effective training so that any evaluation will show positive results.

## Ten Requirements for an Effective Training Program

### 1. Base the program on the needs of the participants.

This is the most fundamental of the ten requirements. If the program does not meet participants' needs, the results of evaluating might be disastrous.

There are a number of ways to determine needs. Some of the more practical approaches are as follows:

- Ask the participants themselves. This can be done through a survey asking them what knowledge and/or skills they feel they need to do their jobs better. (See pages 16–19 for details.)
- Ask the managers of the participants what knowledge and/or skills they think their subordinates need. Not only will this provide valuable information to consider in planning the curriculum, but it will also help to create a relationship with the managers regarding their acceptance and support of the

program. And this is important in giving them a feeling of "ownership" regarding the program.

- Ask their subordinates what knowledge, skills, and/or attitudes they think their supervisors need. This is obviously an approach that is risky, as those of you familiar with "360 degree feedback" know. Many supervisors don't appreciate "criticism" from subordinates. You can call it suggestions, but any suggestion is telling the person what to do or what to quit doing. And no matter how tactfully it is offered with a sincere desire to be helpful, there is a good chance that it will be taken as criticism and resented. This is obviously not true of all supervisors but is frequent enough to suggest caution. Having said that, 360 degree feedback done in the right way and in the right culture is an extremely effective (level 3) evaluation methodology.

- Study the performance appraisals of the participants. This will give you clues as to their strengths and weaknesses. If you are not part of Human Resources, here is where cooperation with that department is important and can be strengthened.

## 2. **Set learning objectives.**

The needs must be converted to objectives that state what participants are expected to learn in the program. We also suggest that you consider developing objectives that reflect expected behavior change on the job. This will help set the table for evaluating level 3 after the course is over, and helps us avoid the tendency to think our jobs stop when participants leave the classroom.

In a training program, an instructor has three possible objectives: to increase knowledge, increase skills, and change attitudes.

For example, if you are teaching Kirkpatrick's "four levels," your learning objectives for Reaction and Learning (the first two levels) might be stated as follows:

1. To describe the meaning of each of the levels
2. To be able to list the guidelines for each level
3. To be able to create a sample form for measuring Reaction
4. To be able to design a test for evaluating Learning
5. To have a desire for implementing one or more of the levels back on the job

You will note that all of these can be accomplished in the training program.

The objectives for Behavior might be

1. to design a Reaction sheet for one program when you get back on the job
2. to develop a pretest and posttest for evaluating Learning on one program
3. to use the Reaction sheet and tests on the next program you will offer

If the program is designed to reduce turnover of new employees, a Results objective might be "to reduce turnover among new employees to 2 percent or less beginning December 1."

### 3. **Schedule the program at the right time.**

At a recent program I conducted in Racine, Wisconsin, I (Don) was asked to teach five 3.5-hour sessions in a weeklong program. In order to do it for all three shifts, I needed to repeat the program each day. The schedule they gave me was to teach the first session from 7:00 to 10:30 A.M. and repeat it from 3:00 to 6:30 P.M. each day. I lived in Milwaukee, about two hours away. It was too far to go home between sessions, and I had trouble finding something to do each day from 10:30 A.M. until 3:00 P.M. This was the worst schedule I ever had in conducting programs. The problem was that they set the schedule and didn't ask me what schedule I would prefer. I would have told them 8:30–noon and 1:00–4:30. And why didn't they ask me? Because my preferred schedule wouldn't meet their need of having the programs at a time convenient for those attending and their bosses sparing them. And this is the way it should be—that programs are scheduled to meet the convenience and needs of the participants and their bosses and not the instructors. If the participants are attending at a bad time as far as they are concerned, their attitude toward the entire program might be negative.

### 4. **Hold the program at the right place with the right amenities.**

Some organizations have their own appropriate facilities. Others need to hold their programs in another location. This is a very important decision because the time and attitudes of the participants must be considered. Travel time must be considered. If the program is going to run for a week, the amount of travel time might not be important. But if it is a program lasting three hours or less, the meeting should be scheduled close to "home." Otherwise, complaining and negative attitudes can result.

I (Don) had a recent experience at a large company in Minneapolis. I was part of a consulting team that did a Leadership program at the home base. I taught one day on "Managing Change." The participants came from all over the country to attend the one-week program.

At the program opening and every day after, food was provided. In the morning, it included cold cereal, English muffins, toast, bagels, fruit, muffins, coffee, decaf, and tea. During the morning break, the supplies were replenished. For lunch, each participant went through the cafeteria and took whatever he or she wished. During the afternoon break, cookies, fruit, coffee, decaf, and cold soft drinks were provided. The participants were on an expense account for evening meals.

The company then made a decision in order to reduce costs. Instead of participants going to Minneapolis, the consulting team went to the locations of the participants. I remember going to Seattle to teach my one day. At the start of the program, no food or drinks were provided, and some of the smarter ones brought their own coffee. At the morning break, the participants were reminded where the vending machines were located. The participants were on their own for lunch, and no refreshments were provided at the afternoon break. This was an obvious attempt to set an example of saving costs.

Was it worth it? There were some participants who had talked with those who attended the program in Minneapolis, where they got the "royal treatment." Possibly, some of them left the program with negative attitudes about the way they were treated, which may have resulted in negative attitudes toward the training department, the program itself, and even a desire to apply what was taught.

## 5. **Invite the right people to attend.**

Who are the right people, and how many can be handled effectively?

The "right people" are those whose needs are met in the program content. Each instructor must decide, "Can I mix levels of employees and have supervisors attend with higher level managers?" The answer lies in the culture of the organization and the attitudes subordinates and bosses have toward each other. In some cases, subordinates would be afraid to speak up because higher level managers are in attendance. On the other hand, some organizations have "families" of levels attending together because they work together on the job.

Another decision must be the size of the group. The answer to this is based on the size of the organization, the size of the facilities, the type of program (presentation or workshop), the cost, and the skill of the leader as trainer and/or facilitator. Some organizations limit attendance to fifteen participants, while others permit 100 or more to attend.

### 6. **Select effective instructors.**

This is probably the most important decision. The qualifications should be the same whether or not the instructor is an inside person or hired from the outside. Obvious qualifications are knowledge of the subject and the ability to communicate effectively. Other necessary qualifications are desire to teach, knowledge of the group, skill in facilitating discussion if a workshop, and ability to establish rapport with the group. If an outside person is selected, cost becomes an important factor.

The best way to decide on an instructor is to see the person in action. This is particularly true if you hire an outside speaker or consultant. When I (Don, again) was in charge of daytime seminars for executives at the Management Institute of the University of Wisconsin, we had a standard of 4.7 out of 5 points on our Reaction sheets. This was a high standard, and we usually lived up to it by carefully selecting leaders. There was one executive from GE who was giving presentations all over the United States. I thought that he must be effective or he wouldn't get so many bookings, so I hired him to conduct a full-day seminar for top executives. I oriented him about the group and agreed with his subject. He would present the program on a Thursday for presidents and vice presidents. On Friday, he would do it for middle- level managers.

I almost wanted to crawl under a chair because he read most of his material and concentrated on the theory and philosophy of GE. It was too late to get him to change, and I doubt if I would have been successful. His ratings both days were 3.4 on a 5 scale and the Reaction sheets were anything but complimentary.

After the second day, he said,

> Don, I notice that you have the participants fill out Reaction sheets. I would like to have you send me a copy because I am always interested in any ideas that I can use to make my presentations more effective. Also, Don, I know that you coordinate many programs. Would you write me a letter and offer any suggestions you have for making my presentations more effective?

I took him at his word and wrote a very tactful letter offering four suggestions:

1. Do not read so much, and maintain eye contact with the group.
2. Use more examples from GE and other organizations.
3. Involve the group by asking them questions to challenge them or having them ask you questions.
4. Prepare handouts for the participants so they won't have to take so many notes. I told him that any program coordinator would be happy to reproduce them for the participants.

This took place in 1979, and I am still waiting for a thank you note. But I did hear in a roundabout way that he told someone that I had written a "nasty" letter and that he would never again participate in a University of Wisconsin program. How right he was! I would certainly never invite him back.

This suggests that when using outside consultants or speakers, be sure that they will be effective. The best way, of course, is to hear them personally. Most of the consulting and speaking work that I do is based on someone actually being at one of my programs. If you can't hear them personally, get recommendations from someone you trust who has seen and heard the person present or lead a workshop. An alternative is to watch them on a DVD of a presentation or workshop.

Using Subject Matter Experts (SMEs) is a common practice these days, and a "best practice" when these experts are properly qualified and trained to deliver training content in an expert manner. Do not assume that because they are content experts, they are also expert trainers. Effective Train the Trainer programs are usually a great investment.

We have one more suggestion. When you as the program coordinator invite speakers or instructors, tell them ahead of time about the Reaction sheets and the standard you expect them to meet. (This assumes that you have established standards for your programs, which we hope you have!) Many times, they will ask for help in preparing for the session because they want to meet or exceed the standard. Then they won't be surprised (or shocked) when they see the Reaction sheets and know whether or not they met the standard.

7. **Use effective techniques and aids.**

Each trainer or facilitator has his or her own approaches and illustrations. Regarding aids, there are three main criteria to consider:

    a. What will help in communicating to the group?
    b. What will help get and control participation?
    c. What will help get and maintain the attention and interest of the participants?

The answer to "a" may include handouts, Microsoft PowerPoint slides, overhead projector transparencies, and/or a flip chart or white board. If the group is large, a microphone may also be needed. My (Don) own personal preferences are overhead projector transparencies, handouts, and a flip chart. I often get teased or criticized for being "behind the times" with my transparencies, but I am comfortable with that method and some participants welcome this aid rather than the PowerPoint slides that they are tired of seeing. If I need a microphone, I like a lavaliere mike so I can move around easily. This is part of my approach to teaching—the PIE approach—Practical, Interactive, and Enjoyable. If you decide to use PowerPoint, be sure that it is not boring to the participants and contributing to "death by PowerPoint."

8. **Accomplish the program objectives.**

Requirement number 2 stated, "Set learning objectives." It is an obvious requirement that those objectives be accomplished.

9. **Satisfy the participants.**

The learning objectives established by the trainers might be accomplished to their satisfaction, but the participants (your customers) may be disappointed with the program. This is where Reaction sheets are important to measure the satisfaction of the participants. When they go back to their jobs, you should be certain that they will be saying positive things about the program. If not, word may get to higher management that the participants say that "the program was a waste of time" or something similar. And this may be all the "evidence" they need to determine that the program was not effective.

10. **Evaluate the program.**

Even though we have listed it last, plans for evaluation should be drawn up before the program is offered. Reaction sheets should be prepared and ready to use. Decisions should be made as to whether to evaluate Learning and for what programs. If a decision is made to evaluate, a pretest may be needed to administer to the participants before the program begins.

To measure Behavior and Results, forms and techniques are typically not needed until some time (three months?) after the program is over. But decisions should be made sooner than that regarding what programs are going to be evaluated at levels 3 and 4. Also, if managers are going to be involved, efforts should be made to contact them in advance to get them to cooperate.

## Summary

Before beginning the evaluation process, be sure you are delivering quality programs. So, consider the requirements listed above to be sure the program is effective.

Then determine how much skill, time, and budget can be devoted to evaluation.

Then consider which programs are the most important to evaluate.

Combine the resources with the programs you consider most important to evaluate, and make the final decisions on what programs should be evaluated and at what levels.

The minimum you should do for all programs is level 1. All this requires is a Reaction (smile) sheet that should be administered at an "instructor-led" program or online for an "e-learning" program.

Chapter 3 gives a number of suggestions of forms and approaches that you can borrow and/or adapt.

Level 2 may require a pretest and posttest approach. Before deciding on what resources you need, carefully read Chapter 4 to see if you can find forms and procedures that you can borrow or adapt.

Then, if necessary, you may be able to find some person in Human Resources or another department who is qualified to develop an appropriate test.

In order to determine what resources you need to evaluate levels 3 and 4, read Chapters 5 and 6 and look for forms and techniques you can borrow. Then determine what additional help is needed.

# Chapter 2

---

# Getting Your Managers
# on Board

Chapter 1 suggested that "the third choice of help" in analyzing your resources is the line managers if they are willing to assist in determining needs and/or evaluating training programs. This chapter will suggest ways to get their cooperation.

We would like to start out by quoting an old friend and writer of several management books. In his book *The Change Resistors,* George Odiorne stated, "If you want people to accept what you have decided, give them a feeling of ownership."

The following example of how I (Don) teach Decision-Making illustrates a way to get that cooperation.

I explain that managers can make decisions four different ways:

1. Make their own decision, and try to sell it to and get cooperation from subordinates in implementing the decision.
2. Ask subordinates, either individually or collectively, for their input before making a decision. Consider the input, and then make the decision and try to get acceptance from the subordinates and cooperation in implementing the decision.
3. Call their subordinates together, present them with the problem, and lead them to a consensus decision. Managers serve as facilitators and agree to implement the decision.
4. Empower subordinates to make the decision and agree to implement it.

When these four ways are analyzed in terms of the "quality" of the decision, there may be no clear-cut difference. The decisions may be either good or bad no matter which approach is used, but the input from more people may increase the chances for a good decision.

When the four ways are analyzed in terms of the "acceptance" of the decision by those involved, it is clear that when proceeding from the first way to the fourth, there would be a clear-cut difference, and acceptance would increase with the amount of "ownership" or involvement.

So, how can managers be given a feeling of "ownership" regarding evaluation?

There are two ways to do it. One way is to get them involved by providing interest and encouragement to their subordinates who attend programs, whether inside or outside the organization. As an example, when I (Don) was with the Management Institute of the University of Wisconsin, I was concerned with the relationship between the supervisors who attend our programs and their bosses. I asked the participants whether their bosses had talked with them before they attended, and the answer was usually "yes." When I asked for details, the typical answer was that they were encouraged to learn what they could and have a good time. I asked them what they expected their bosses to do when they returned to their jobs. The typical answer was that the bosses would tell them that they hoped they had a good time and that there was a lot of work to do.

I (Don) decided to write a short booklet for the managers who were sending the people to our programs. I suggested that managers do the following.

## Before the Program

Preview the program with them, and show an interest in the content. Tell them to learn what they can and to come back with a list of any practical ideas that you can implement together.

Also, consider asking them to prepare a brief summary of what they learned that they can share with their colleagues. (As we know from adult theory, an excellent way to increase learning is to teach someone else what you have learned.) Tell them to have a good time and that you will take care of their job while they are gone.

This approach will be a motivating factor in getting them to learn practical ideas to take back to the job.

## During the Program

If the program consists of a number of sessions spread over a period of time, it would be a good idea for the manager to discuss each session with the participant by asking such questions as

How is the meeting going?
Have you picked up any ideas we can work together to implement?

Another idea is to ask qualified managers to serve as trainers or facilitators to get them on board.

## After the Program

Take time when they return to go over the ideas they brought home and work out any ideas for improving performance. Specifically, focus on learnings that can be transferred into productive new behaviors on the job. The more relevant the material, the more time should be spent making sure it is leveraged for the good of the organization.

We think that the approaches described above are very important in getting maximum benefits from training programs and getting managers to feel that they are an important part.

We have suggested these approaches to many groups where we have made presentations. We have asked for those who have used them to raise their hands. And only a few hands go up. We have encouraged the others to give them a try.

It is easy to say, "Get the managers and supervisors to do this or that," but a real challenge is to find the triggers that will actually make it happen. We have found that the best way to do this is to show them what their investment will do. Jim likes to talk about the "missing link" between training and results. It is the reinforcement of new behaviors on the job. Explain to them that training in and of itself is of limited value. Also, emphasize that the learning of knowledge and skills is of equally limited value unless ways are found to get participants to transfer those learnings to key behaviors. And that is where the managers need to come front and center. It is highly unlikely that even a small percentage of participants of any program will, on their own, find the time and motivation to implement new behaviors successfully. Only through application of targeted support and accountability by supervisors and managers will that actually happen. The big "punch line" here is that if those mission-critical behaviors do not become business as usual, in all probability the expected results from the training will never materialize. Chapter 5 on Behavior will describe various ways to do this, as does our book, *Transferring Learning to Behavior*.

Another way to get them on board is to ask them to participate in determining the training content. For example, most organizations have training programs for supervisors. The program content is usually prepared by curriculum designers and the trainers with little or no input from the supervisors and their bosses. The curriculum designers may have informally asked for their input but not in a specific way. In some organizations, they survey supervisors and ask such questions as "What kinds of programs do you want to attend that will help you do your job better?" They do not do it in a way that the responses could be tabulated and analyzed.

We suggest the following approach to get those attending as well as their bosses involved:

1. Develop a list of all the possible subjects you are able to offer supervisors.
2. Design a form and get their input by reacting to each possible topic.
3. Tabulate the responses and rank them in order.
4. Get responses from their bosses regarding the benefit of each topic to their subordinates, the supervisors.
5. Tabulate the responses and rank them in order.
6. Compare the two rank orders.
7. Tentatively plan the curriculum, considering the results of the surveys as well as the input from the training professionals.
8. Select a Training Advisory Committee of middle- and upper-level managers.

9. Show this committee the results of your survey and the tentative program you have designed. Get their input and consider it.

10. Finalize the curriculum.

See Exhibit 2.1 for a suggested form to be completed by supervisors.

All the returns would be tabulated, and the following weights given:

A weight of 2 would be given for each X in the first column.
A weight of 1 would be given for each X in the second column.
A weight of 0 would be given for each X in the third column.

From these tabulations, a total weight and rank order would be obtained.

The same form can be used for the managers (bosses of those attending) with the following instruction:

"Please put an X after each statement to indicate your analysis of the supervisors' (your subordinates) need for each subject."

It is probably obvious that the results of the survey of supervisors would be different than that of their bosses on some items. The responses from the supervisors are "felt needs," while the responses of the bosses are "observed needs."

For example, where I (Don) have used the survey, there was general agreement that the most practical programs were how to motivate employees, how to manage change, decision-making and empowerment, leadership styles and application, building teamwork, and how to train employees.

The topics on which there was the greatest degree of disagreement were diversity in the workforce, performance appraisal, total quality improvement, safety, and housekeeping.

The question to be considered is to whom should these results be communicated? We feel there is no secret about the results, so each training department can decide for themselves. If they see benefit in communicating to those who completed the form, they should do it. For sure, it should be communicated to the Training Advisory Committee to demonstrate that you want to meet the needs of the participants and to give them a chance to comment.

Trainers and curriculum designers who will decide on the

Exhibit 2.1. Determining Training Needs

These are possible training topics that may be of help to you in doing your job. Please place an X after each topic to indicate how much need you have for that topic. Your responses will help us develop an effective training program.

| POSSIBLE TOPICS | Great need | Some need | No need |
|---|---|---|---|
| 1.  Diversity in the workforce | | | |
| 2.  How to motivate employees | | | |
| 3.  Interpersonal communications | | | |
| 4.  Written communications | | | |
| 5.  Oral communications | | | |
| 6.  How to manage time | | | |
| 7.  How to delegate effectively | | | |
| 8.  Planning and organizing work | | | |
| 9.  Handling complaints and/or grievances | | | |
| 10. How to manage change | | | |
| 11. Decision-making and empowerment | | | |
| 12. Leadership styles and application | | | |
| 13. Performance appraisal | | | |
| 14. Coaching and counseling | | | |
| 15. How to conduct productive meetings | | | |
| 16. Building teamwork | | | |
| 17. How to discipline | | | |
| 18. Total quality improvement | | | |
| 19. Safety | | | |
| 20. Housekeeping | | | |
| 21. How to improve morale | | | |
| 22. How to reward performance | | | |
| 23. How to train employees | | | |
| 24. How to reduce absenteeism and tardiness | | | |
| 25. How to use the computer | | | |

program content would look for items of agreement and discuss those items where there is quite a difference of opinion. Here is where the input from the Training Advisory Committee of higher management would be considered. This involvement would give them a "feeling of ownership" that would be important in getting them to accept the program. It would also add another dimension to consider when making the final decision on the curriculum.

In making a final decision on content, the various sources to be considered would include the trainees, their bosses, the Training Advisory Committee, the curriculum designers, and those who will do the training. The final decision would be made by the training department.

Once training topics are determined, it may be possible to get managers to act as subject matter experts to get their input on specific program content. It would be wise to ask them what kinds of new behaviors they would like to see their direct reports perform on the job as well as the types of skills they will need to develop in order to perform their jobs more effectively. The more helpful input they provide to the course developers, the more likely they are to support on-the-job application of new learnings.

These and other approaches of getting all levels of management involved would accomplish several things. It would communicate clearly that the training professionals are eager to present practical programs that meet the needs of management. It also gives all levels of management a feeling of "ownership" that is important to the acceptance of the training department and the programs themselves. Finally, it provides assurance that the program does meet the needs of those attending.

Another way of utilizing managers and supervisors is to get them involved in the actual delivery of the course. This is particularly effective with programs that have to do with leadership and coaching. After all, that is their job, and who better to hear it from than those who do it? Some words of caution, however. A good supervisor or manager may not be an effective trainer and may not be enthusiastic about teaching. After selecting those with desire and potential, you must provide some "train the trainer" preparation for them prior to their doing the actual training. You may have the staff do it, or you may have to call on an outside consultant. And you must orient them on the participants as well as the program objectives.

Another idea is to get a member of upper management to intro-
duce the course and encourage the participants to learn and use the
learning to improve performance.

This approach of getting all levels of management involved in planning and presenting the training programs would accomplish several
things. It would communicate clearly that the training professionals
are eager to present practical programs that meet the needs of management. It would give all levels of management a feeling of ownership that is important to the acceptance of the training department
and the programs themselves. It would also give assurance that the
program does meet the needs of those attending.

An example from my experience illustrates a word of caution about
involving the managers in teaching all or part of a course. Some time
ago, I (Don) was asked by the Training Director of a large Milwaukee
company to prepare a lesson plan of fifteen hours for a basic course on
Leadership and Human Relations for their first-level supervisors and
foremen. So I did it and included subject content, handouts, material,
audiovisual aids, and two case studies to use with role playing. I presented the lesson plan to him and asked, "Who will teach the course?"

I was surprised and shocked to hear him say, "The instructors will
all be line managers. After all, they supervise the trainees, so they
should teach them what they are expected to do on the job."

After gathering my breath, I told him that if he only used managers
and no professional trainers, the least he should do is to have me go
over the lesson plan with them and provide some suggestions on
teaching techniques. I wanted to tell him that it would be a terrible
mistake because most of them would be neither qualified nor interested, and that they would probably feel like fools getting up in front
of their subordinates and trying to teach subject matter prepared by
someone else. Fortunately, for him and the corporation, the program
was never implemented.

One of my (Don) most memorable positive experiences was an
invitation from Dave Harris, the Industrial Relations Manager of
A.O. Smith Corporation in Milwaukee, to present a basic supervisory
program to all their foremen and supervisors. So I developed a series
of five 3-hour sessions covering such subjects as Leadership, Communication, Motivation, Discipline, Managing Change, and Decision-
Making. After showing him the lesson plan, I asked him if he could
get the top management group in manufacturing to attend a capsule

program of three to six hours that I would like to give them for their reaction and approval. He said, "I'll try."

He was successful, so I presented the program to the eight top-level managers (including the Vice President of Manufacturing) at the Milwaukee Athletic Club instead of at their training facility. (Do you suppose they didn't want the lower-level managers to know they were going to attend a training program? I wonder.)

The group was happy with the program and offered a few minor suggestions. I asked them before they left, "I will present the program to all your first-level supervisors and foremen as Dave suggested. But what about their bosses, the superintendents and general foremen? Would it be a good idea to give it to them before presenting it to their subordinates?"

I held my breath waiting for the answer. Almost immediately, the Vice President of Manufacturing said, "Why don't you give the whole course to them, as you suggested?" Dave and I agreed, and it was done.

I can't tell you what a difference that decision made in dollars or attitude benefits, but it was great. From the supervisors and foremen's standpoint, it was the fact that the bosses were setting an example instead of just telling their subordinates to attend. And the fact that both levels got the same training would greatly enhance the chances of on-the-job application.

The A.O. Smith example reminds me of my teaching at the Management Institute of the University of Wisconsin. When I (Don) first started there as a trainer, we conducted a series of programs only for first-level foremen and supervisors. We received many suggestions (complaints?) from them that "our bosses should be here!"

So we presented a series of programs for department heads, general foremen, and superintendents. And those attending told us, "The plant managers should be here and get this training too." So we set up a series of six 1-day conferences for them. And, you guessed it. They said that the ones who really need it are the presidents and vice presidents, so we set up a series of Executive Seminars.

All of the programs were successful in terms of attendance and quality.

Think about your own approach to selecting trainees. Are you considering all levels of management? Keep in mind that upper management must set an example by being willing to learn as well by being effective leaders.

The final challenge is to get managers involved in the evaluation process. This will be addressed in Chapters 5 and 6 dealing with Behavior and Results.

## Summary

The challenge for training professionals is to get managers involved not only in the training itself but also in the evaluation process. In the training process, they can be helpful in determining subject content and possibly teaching part of the program. This will give them a feeling of ownership that is so important in getting their acceptance and cooperation.

They should also be involved in encouraging and helping the trainees (their subordinates) apply what they learned by providing support and accountability.

The third challenge is to get them to assist in the evaluation process of measuring levels 3 and 4. This will be described in detail in Chapters 5 and 6.

Training professionals have no control over the managers and the trainees when they leave the classroom. Therefore, trainers need to use influence to get managers on board to assist in the planning, implementation, and evaluation of the training programs.

# Chapter 3

# Implementing Level 1: Reaction

I (Don) was surprised and upset by an article in the August 2006 issue of *Training* magazine. The title of the article was "Are You Too Nice to Train?" The opening read,

> Remember that mean, crabby teacher in high school? We do too. Although you hate to admit it, chances are you learned a lot in his or her class. When it comes to effective training, positive smile-sheet evaluations often mean negative results. In the classroom, kindness may only get you so far. And a little evaluation can be a dangerous thing.

The article goes on to quote research, based mostly on education programs where grades are given, that smile sheets do more harm than good. Another section is headed "Why Smiley Sheets Stink." One statement says, "Some people like courses where they learn almost nothing. In fact there is evidence that some people leave training courses knowing significantly less about something than they did when they started the course, and yet they sometimes like the unlearning experience."

I guess the part of the article that bothered me most was called "The Games Trainers Play." It described how trainers were only concerned about how they were rated and not about the other important factors to be evaluated. It stated that giving out candy, food, and prizes and telling engaging stories are just a few of the many tactics trainers use in order to influence their level 1 scores. To get good smile-sheet scores, some trainers use "voice tricks," while others go out of their way to compliment the intelligence of their students, often thanking them for a great class.

And their comment sheets ask nothing about the practical nature of the program and other factors that are important, only about them. To summarize, the obvious purpose of the article was to say that Reaction (smile) sheets are not worth anything regarding the effectiveness of the training. In fact, they may do more harm than good. And, by the way, there were some misquotes in the article, including one or two by my son, Jim, who was interviewed at length. Only a few of his positive comments were included.

*Note:* A rebuttal article by me was printed in the October issue. I was surprised and thankful that the editor printed it.

The terms "smile sheets" or "happiness ratings" are used by some trainers to refer to Reaction sheets. I think they are correct. But, I don't like the tone as described in the *Training* article when they use these words. It sounds like they are saying they aren't of any value and may do more harm than good.

We define Reaction sheets as "measures of customer satisfaction." And this puts emphasis on their importance and value. Trainees are really your customers, whether or not they pay for the program. When I (Don) worked for the Management Institute of the University of Wisconsin, those who attended our conferences and seminars were paying customers. And our existence depended on their reaction. Sometimes, a high-level manager would attend to appraise the course and decide whether or not to send supervisors. A positive reaction of that manager was critical.

We offered a ten-day certificate with two programs of five days each. The programs were separated by several months. The reaction of the participants to the first half of the program determined whether or not they came back for the second half.

The first reason for Reaction sheets is to know how the customers feel about the program and to make whatever changes are necessary to improve it.

There is another reason why Reaction sheets (or e-mail forms) are important. If the trainers do not ask for them, the trainees are subtly told that the trainers know what they are doing and need no feedback from the trainees regarding the effectiveness of the program. Trainees may not like that. So, Reaction sheets should be used for *every program*.

Here are the guidelines we recommend for developing a form that will get maximum information in the minimum time needed to complete the form.

1. Make a list of the items where you want feedback. We suggest from eight to fifteen items.
2. Design a form where the reactions can be quantified. The most common forms are on a 5-point scale using either *Excellent, Very good, Good, Fair,* and *Poor* or the well-known Likert scale, *Strongly agree, Agree, Neutral, Disagree,* and *Strongly disagree.* We don't have any preference for starting with the positive or the negative term. Allow room for comments.
3. End the form asking for suggestions for improvement.
4. Do not ask trainees to sign or put their names on the forms. In some cases, you may want to say that a signature is optional in case someone makes a suggestion you may want to pursue.
5. Try to get a 100 percent response at the conclusion of the program. If evaluating e-learning, make it easy to respond and stress the importance of a 100 percent response. If evaluating an instructor-led program, give them time to fill out the form and lay it on the back table as they leave.

Our job is to provide a number of different approaches for developing a form and suggesting one other approach that can be used for measuring Reaction. We will first offer five forms that we have developed and a unique one we found abroad. We will then reproduce the forms from case studies in the third edition of *Evaluating Training Programs: The Four Levels*.

Your job is to sort through the forms and "borrow" or develop your own. If you want to develop one and have me critique it, you can send it to Don.

The first four forms could be used or adapted for any program. Exhibit 3.5 is a true "smile sheet" that we found in a restaurant in Geneva, Switzerland. Exhibit 3.6 would be especially useful if you have a number of trainers or facilitators and don't want to use a separate form for each one.

The remainder of the chapter will include various forms from the case studies in the third edition of *Evaluating Training Programs: The Four Levels*. Because of the title and content of the Duke Energy case study, we have included a fairly complete description of the design and use of their Reaction form.

Exhibit 3.1. Reaction Sheet

---

Please give us your frank reactions and comments. They will help us to evaluate this program and improve future programs.

Leader _____    Subject _____

1.  How do you rate the subject? (interest, benefit, etc.)

    _____ Excellent                Comments and suggestions:

    _____ Very good

    _____ Good

    _____ Fair

    _____ Poor

2.  How do you rate the conference leader? (knowledge of subject matter, ability to communicate, etc.)

    _____ Excellent                Comments and suggestions:

    _____ Very good

    _____ Good

    _____ Fair

    _____ Poor

3.  How do you rate the facilities? (comfort, convenience, etc.)

    _____ Excellent                Comments and suggestions:

    _____ Very good

    _____ Good

    _____ Fair

    _____ Poor

4.  How do you rate the schedule?

    _____ Excellent                Comments and suggestions:

    _____ Very good

    _____ Good

    _____ Fair

    _____ Poor

5.  What would have improved the program?

---

Exhibit 3.2. Reaction Sheet

---

Leader _____     Subject _____

1. How pertinent was the subject to your needs and interests?

   _____ Not at all _____ To some extent _____ Very much

2. How was the ratio of presentation to discussion?

   _____ Too much presentation _____ Okay _____ Too much discussion

3. How do you rate the instructor?

| | Excellent | Very good | Good | Fair | Poor |
|---|---|---|---|---|---|
| a. In stating objectives | | | | | |
| b. In keeping the session alive and interesting | | | | | |
| c. In communicating | | | | | |
| d. In using aids | | | | | |
| e. In maintaining a friendly and helpful attitude | | | | | |

4. What is your overall rating of the leader?

   _____ Excellent                Comments and suggestions:

   _____ Very good

   _____ Good

   _____ Fair

   _____ Poor

5. What would have made the session more effective?

---

Exhibit 3.3. Reaction Sheet

---

In order to determine the effectiveness of the program in meeting your needs and interests, we need your input. Please give us your reactions, and make any comments or suggestions that will help us to serve you.

*Instructions:* Please circle the appropriate response after each statement.

|  | *Strongly disagree* | | *Neutral* | | | *Strongly agree* | |
|---|---|---|---|---|---|---|---|
| 1. The material covered in the program was relevant to my job. | 1 2 | 3 | 4 5 | 6 | 7 8 | | |
| 2. The material was presented in an interesting way. | 1 2 | 3 | 4 5 | 6 | 7 8 | | |
| 3. The instructor was an effective communicator. | 1 2 | 3 | 4 5 | 6 | 7 8 | | |
| 4. The instructor was well prepared. | 1 2 | 3 | 4 5 | 6 | 7 8 | | |
| 5. The audiovisual aids were effective. | 1 2 | 3 | 4 5 | 6 | 7 8 | | |
| 6. The handouts will be of help to me. | 1 2 | 3 | 4 5 | 6 | 7 8 | | |
| 7. I will be able to apply much of the material to my job. | 1 2 | 3 | 4 5 | 6 | 7 8 | | |
| 8. The facilities were suitable. | 1 2 | 3 | 4 5 | 6 | 7 8 | | |
| 9. The schedule was suitable. | 1 2 | 3 | 4 5 | 6 | 7 8 | | |
| 10. There was a good balance between presentation and group involvement. | 1 2 | 3 | 4 5 | 6 | 7 8 | | |
| 11. I feel that the workshop will help me do my job better. | 1 2 | 3 | 4 5 | 6 | 7 8 | | |

What would have improved the program?

Exhibit 3.4. Reaction Sheet

---

Please complete this form to let us know your reaction to the program. Your input will help us to evaluate our efforts, and your comments and suggestions will help us to plan future programs that meet your needs and interests.

*Instructions:* Please circle the appropriate number after each statement and then add your comments.

|  | *High* |  |  |  | *Low* |
|---|---|---|---|---|---|
| 1. How do you rate the subject content? (interesting, helpful, etc.) | 5 | 4 | 3 | 2 | 1 |

Comments:

| 2. How do you rate the instructor? (preparation, communication, etc.) | 5 | 4 | 3 | 2 | 1 |
|---|---|---|---|---|---|

Comments:

| 3. How do you rate the facilities? (comfort, convenience, etc.) | 5 | 4 | 3 | 2 | 1 |
|---|---|---|---|---|---|

Comments:

| 4. How do you rate the schedule? (time, length, etc.) | 5 | 4 | 3 | 2 | 1 |
|---|---|---|---|---|---|

Comments:

| 5. How would you rate the program as an educational experience to help you do your job better? | 5 | 4 | 3 | 2 | 1 |
|---|---|---|---|---|---|

6. What topics were most beneficial?

7. What would have improved the program?

---

Exhibit 3.5. Reaction Sheet

Dear Client,

We would like to have your comments and suggestions to enable us to offer you the kind of service you would like.

Would you help us by ticking the face that is most indicative of your feelings:

| ☐ **breakfast** | ☐ **lunch** | *Very good* | *Good* | *Average* |

1.  Are you satisfied with the quality of the meals?

2.  Are you satisfied with the variety of dishes available?

3.  Do you find our prices competitive?

4.  What do you think of the service?

5.  How do you find the atmosphere in the restaurant?

6.  Suggestions:

Name: _____

Address: _____

Exhibit 3.6. Reaction Sheet

---

Please give your frank and honest reactions. Insert the appropriate number.

Scale:    5 = Excellent    4 = Very good    3 = Good    2 = Fair    1 = Poor

| *Leader* | *Subject* | *Presentation* | *Discussion* | *Audiovisual aids* | *Overall* |
|---|---|---|---|---|---|
| Tom Jones | | | | | |
| Gerald Ford | | | | | |
| Luis Aparicio | | | | | |
| Simon Bolivar | | | | | |
| Muhammad Ali | | | | | |
| Chris Columbus | | | | | |
| Bart Starr | | | | | |

Facilities   Rating _____              Meals   Rating _____

Comments:                                  Comments:

Schedule   Rating _____             Overall program   Rating _____

Comments:                                  Comments:

What would have improved the program?

---

# Developing an Effective Level 1 Reaction Form

## Duke Energy Corporation
## W. Derrick Allman
## Plan, Manage, and Procure Training Services
## Charlotte, North Carolina

In this case study, Allman described in detail the development of the form (Exhibit 3.8) and the way it was used. Following is a summary of the case study.

Reaction sheets indicate the mood of participants as they leave training. The goal of level 1 evaluations is to "measure participant's perception (reaction) to learning experiences relative to a course, content, instructor, and relevancy to job immediately following the experience in order to initiate continuous improvement of training experiences." As a result, our project established three primary objectives:

1. Questions developed for the reaction-level evaluation *must* measure the course, content, instructor, and relevancy to the job. These are four areas considered essential to successful training programs.
2. The form and delivery of the level 1 evaluation must communicate a link between quality, process improvement, and action. Participants *must* be made to feel as though their individual response is a factor in the continuous improvement process.
3. Action plans should be initiated to address identified weaknesses without regard to owner, political correctness, or other bias. If the results indicate poor quality, then appropriate corrective action should be taken. If excellence is indicated in an unlikely place, then reward and celebration should be offered commensurate with the accomplishment.

In addition to the primary objectives, several other objectives evolved. First was the need to identify the prerequisite processes that must be accomplished with each learning event. It became evident that the success of the level 1 process is directly linked to the proper completion of prerequisites for a course. Second, postmeasurement activities should be addressed by subsequent teams. During the initial database design, the team knew that certain reports would be required and others desired. Most reports were prepared during the first phase of development.

The initial computer project deliverables included the following:

- Proposed questions to be included on the level 1 evaluation
- Proposed measures from which management would determine actions to be taken when analyzing evaluation results
- Recommendations for deployment of the process within

Exhibit 3.7. Reaction Sheet

---

Please complete the following form by indicating your agreement with each of the statements: *Strongly agree, Agree, Neutral, Disagree,* and *Strongly disagree.*

|  | SA | A | N | D | SD |
|---|---|---|---|---|---|
| 1. My impression of the course was "excellent." | — | — | — | — | — |
| 2. The course objectives were clearly stated in understandable terms. | — | — | — | — | — |
| 3. This course met the defined objectives. | — | — | — | — | — |
| 4. The facility met all needs of the course. | — | — | — | — | — |
| 5. The equipment met all needs of the course. | — | — | — | — | — |
| 6. The course materials were easy to follow. | — | — | — | — | — |
| 7. The course materials were useful. | — | — | — | — | — |
| 8. The instructor(s) demonstrated thorough knowledge of the subject. | — | — | — | — | — |
| 9. The instructor(s) presented information in a clear, understandable manner. | — | — | — | — | — |
| 10. The instructor(s) presented information in a professional manner. | — | — | — | — | — |
| 11. The amount of time scheduled was exactly what was needed to meet the course objectives. | — | — | — | — | — |
| 12. This course relates directly to my job responsibilities. | — | — | — | — | — |
| 13. I would recommend this course to other teammates. | — | — | — | — | — |

corporate training and education, including roles and responsibilities

- Guideline for data collection, cycle times, reports, and analysis of data
- Schedule for developing, delivering, and measuring responsiveness of participants (generic level 1 assessment)
- Database and input program for manually gathering data

Exhibit 3.8. Tabulating Responses to Reaction Sheets

---

Please give us your frank reactions and comments. They will help us to evaluate this program and improve future programs.

Leader ___*Tom Jones*___                    Subject ___*Leadership*___

1.  How do you rate the subject? (interest, benefit, etc.)

    __10__ Excellent              Comments and suggestions:

    __5__ Very good

    __3__ Good                    Rating = *4.1*

    __1__ Fair

    __1__ Poor

2.  How do you rate the conference leader? (knowledge of subject matter, ability to communicate, etc.)

    __8__ Excellent               Comments and suggestions:

    __4__ Very good

    __5__ Good                    Rating = *3.8*

    __2__ Fair

    __1__ Poor

3.  How do you rate the facilities? (comfort, convenience, etc.)

    __7__ Excellent               Comments and suggestions:

    __7__ Very good

    __5__ Good                    Rating = *4.0*

    __1__ Fair

    __0__ Poor

4.  What would have improved the program?

---

*Note:* Ratings are on a 5-point scale.

- Plans and scope document detailing a second (phase 2) project for automating the data acquisition process (This document should include plans for using data collected in multiple ways—that is, requirements that header data be used to confirm enrollment and attendance, automated course completion, level 1 automated analysis and reporting, and so on.)

Along with the development of the computer program, a team worked on drafting an initial set of questions for the standard level 1 Reaction sheets. See Exhibit 3.7 for the form we developed, and Exhibit 3.8 for an example of how to tabulate responses.

This team worked on the draft and completion of a standardized level 1 evaluation form through the spring of 1997 and presented this to the larger body for use in April 1997. We immediately set about the task of piloting the standard questions within our companies and continue to gather data for comparison at this time. In addition, the team is now completing work on the development of level 3 questions for use by the members. As a result of this effort, for the first time a standard set of data will be able to be analyzed in gauging the success of programs that literally span the globe. In doing so, the lessons learned from similar experiences will help in identifying successful practices and in avoiding the pitfalls that others experience.

Duke Energy Training stands at the threshold of a new era in evaluating the effectiveness of training. As we continue to analyze the reactions people have toward training, we are beginning to see indications that suggest a direct correlation between reaction (level 1) and transfer to the job (level 3). If this correlation is correct, the use of sophisticated techniques for analyzing participant reaction will be warranted. On the other hand, if all we are able to glean from the data are indications of areas needing improvement, then we will still be able to implement corrective actions in programs. When used effectively, analysis of level 1 evaluation data can help in the early detection of areas that need improvement or support the conclusion that a good result was achieved.

The remainder of this chapter will show the reaction forms and approaches used in the other case studies.

---

# Evaluating a Leadership Development Program

U.S. Geological Survey
Walden Consulting
Granville, Ohio
Dr. Abram W. Kaplan, Principal Investigator
Jordan Mora, Gillian Poe, Jennifer Altzner,
and Laura Rech
Reston, Virginia

Each Leadership course we offer includes extensive course evaluation materials by participants, both at the module level and for the entire course. In the 101 course (our basic course on leadership), for instance, each of the fourteen modules is assessed with these questions, asked in a daily "green sheet" form:

1. How would you rate the session overall? (1 = Disappointing; 5 = Outstanding)
2. How much of the session's content could you relate back to your duties at work? (1 = Not much; 5 = Very much)
3. On a scale from 1 to 5, with 5 being Outstanding, how would you rate the session's instructor(s)? Preparation? Presentation? Inspiration? Overall?
4. What suggestions would you offer for future improvements of this session?
5. What parts of this session did you find most useful for the future?

These are contained in a half-sheet section. Then, at the end of the week, our level 1 forms ask the following:

1. How would you rate the course overall? (1 = Disappointing; 5 = Outstanding)
2. How valuable was this course to your development as a leader within the USGS? (1 = Not valuable; 5 = Very valuable)
3. What suggestions would you offer for future improvements of this course?

4. What element(s) of this course did you find most useful?
5. Additional comments or suggestions? Thank you!

We complement in-class course evaluations with questionnaire items in our pre-201 surveys asking participants for longer range recollections of the 101 class, and these measures provide a valuable check on the immediate reactions during the workshop.

---

# Developing a Training Program
# for Nonexempt Employees

### First Union National Bank
### Patrick O'Hara, Assistant Vice President
### Human Resources Division, Training and Development
### First Union National Bank
### Charlotte, North Carolina

## CARE

A major goal of First Union is to let employees know how much they and their contribution to the success and growth of First Union are valued. Personal development is one strategy.

CARE is a program that was developed to provide a developmental opportunity for the nonexempt employees who historically have not been the focus of personal development training. As the corporation has expanded over the last several years, there has been tremendous change and upheaval. During mergers and consolidations, employees have the pressures that all this change has brought to bear. CARE is a one-day program devoted to the bank's largest population, the nonexempt employees who have shouldered major responsibilities throughout this growth cycle at First Union.

CARE is an acronym for Communication, Awareness, Renewal, and Empowerment. The learning objectives are to

- increase self-awareness by use of self-assessment tools and group feedback.
- increase understanding of communication styles and develop flexibility in one's own communication style.
- increase communication effectiveness by exposure to and practice in assertiveness concepts and skills.
- understand and implement the steps of goal setting as a tool in career renewal.

Exhibit 3.9. CARE Evaluation Form, National Computer Systems

---

Name of Instructor _____

Location _____

Date _____

National Computer Systems

*Instructions:* When marking each answer:

- Use a No. 2 pencil only.
- Circle appropriate number.
- Cleanly erase any marks you wish to change.

Please use the following scale to record your thoughts about the course content:

1 = *Disagree strongly*
2 = *Disagree*
3 = *Neither agree nor disagree*
4 = *Agree*
5 = *Agree strongly*

**Content**

1. The skills taught in this class are relevant to my personal development.     1  2  3  4  5

2. This class helped me develop those skills.     1  2  3  4  5

3. The material was clearly organized.     1  2  3  4  5

4. The course content met my needs.     1  2  3  4  5

5. Comments:

**Instruction**

*The course instructor*

6. Facilitated class discussions effectively.     1  2  3  4  5

7. Listened carefully to participants.     1  2  3  4  5

8. Assisted in linking concepts to actual interpersonal situations.     1  2  3  4  5

(continued)

Exhibit 3.9. CARE Evaluation Form, National Computer Systems (*continued*)

9. Had excellent presentation skills.              1     2     3     4     5

10. Comments:

*Overall*

11. Rank your overall satisfaction with the program.   1     2     3     4     5

Thank you for taking the time to give constructive feedback on this course. Your responses will be used to improve future courses.

---

---

# Evaluating an Information Technology Skills Training Program

The Regence Group
James C. Baker, E-Learning Specialist
Organizational Development
Portland, Oregon

Immediately after each class on information technology skills, participants launched our Part A online assessment of level 1 and level 2. In Exhibit 3.10 of this case study, you can see the multilevel Part A evaluation tool that we adopted from the American Society for Training and Development (ASTD) and then supplemented with other questions for reporting. Part A questions consisted of a 1–5 (low to high) scale to measure reactions to statements about these categories:

- administration and logistics (prerequisites, facilities, and equipment)
- content (understood the objectives, and the objectives were met)
- design (method of delivery, materials, length of class time, and organization)

- instruction (satisfaction with instructor)
- perceived impact (knowledge and skills increased, applicability to current job, applicability for preparing participant for other jobs in the company, and training that helped toward other jobs in the company)
- overall satisfaction with the class

Exhibit 3.10. Online Assessment of Level 1

---

INSTRUCTIONS: When you have completed this evaluation, click Submit.

Class name and course objectives

Your name:

Instructor name:

Questions

Choices: a. Strongly agree  b. Agree  c. Neither  d. Disagree  e. Strongly disagree

1. I had the knowledge and/or skills required to start this course.
2. The facilities and equipment were favorable to learning.
3. I was able to take this course when I needed it.
4. I clearly understood the course objectives.
5. The course met all of its stated objectives.
6. The way this course was delivered (such as classroom, computer, and video) was an effective way for me to learn this subject matter.
7. Participant materials (handouts, workbooks, etc.) were useful during the course.
8. I had enough time to learn the subject matter covered in the course.
9. The course content was logically organized.
10. I had an opportunity to give input to the course design or content.
11. Overall, I was satisfied with the instructor(s).
12. My knowledge and/or skills increased as a result of this course.
13. The knowledge and/or skills gained through this course are directly applicable to my job.
14. This course has helped prepare me for other job opportunities within the company or industry.
15. Overall, I was satisfied with this course.

---

# Evaluating the Four Levels
# Using a New Assessment Process

Army and Air Force Exchange Service (AAFES)
Steven Jablonski, Educational Support Manager
Dallas, Texas

AAFES Corporate University has developed a plan to integrate Kirkpatrick's four levels of evaluation with current technology available within the company. This plan focuses on upgrading data collection methods for level 1 and level 3 evaluations in 2005.

Under the leadership and guidance of LaSharnda Beckwith, Vice President of Learning, more emphasis is being placed on the assessment process. In the past, individual instructors were responsible for gathering and analyzing the feedback provided by the associates who attended training. LaSharnda has adopted a more structured and uniform approach to the assessment process by establishing a team that is dedicated to the development and analysis of all of Corporate University's assessment efforts.

The Educational Support Team, directed by Steve Jablonski, was formed in late 2004. After analyzing the current assessment process and exploring several different options for administering assessments, Steve's team selected an online option to facilitate the administration of assessments within AAFES. The Microsoft Office SharePoint Portal Server 2003 was launched companywide in 2004. This tool provides a survey feature that Corporate University can use to administer assessments and obtain feedback from the associates who attend courses. The web portal also provides the ability to run reports through Excel spreadsheets and convert the data to an Access database for more detailed analysis. All of these efforts would be more labor-intensive without the aid of this online tool.

The plan for the newly established assessment process is that it will evaluate all classroom courses taught by the Corporate University staff during the 2005 training season. These will include courses such as Basic Project Management, The Manager's Mind-Set, Goal Setting in AAFES, Operational Management, Advanced

Exhibit 3.11 Reaction Sheet

| Course Title | Date | Instructor |
|---|---|---|
| Location | Your Job Title | Your Grade |

**Directions:** Please take a few minutes and give us your evaluation of the training program you completed. We want to know how useful this program will be to you on your job and if changes should be made to the content. This information is for statistical purposes only and we ask that you be honest when answering. After completion, return all evaluations to HQ AAFES HR-U.

Enter the number of the rating which best describes each statement listed below using the following scale.

**4-Strongly Agree     3-Agree     2-Disagree     1-Strongly Disagree**
**0-Not Applicable**

| CONTENT | RATING |
|---|---|
| 1. The content of the course matched the stated objectives. | |
| 2. The difficulty level was about right for me (neither too difficult, nor too easy). | |
| 3. The exercises and examples were realistic and true-to-life. | |
| 4. The instructional methods (lecture, discussion, role-play, etc.) were effective. | |
| 5. What was the weakest part of the course and how could it be improved? | |

| RELEVANCE TO MY JOB | RATING |
|---|---|
| 1. The skills/knowledge taught in this course were applicable to my job. | |
| 2. This course will help me do my job better. | |

| LEARNING MATERIALS | RATING |
|---|---|
| 1. The printed material was easy to read and understand. | |
| 2. The workbooks/handouts were well organized. | |
| 3. I can use the printed material given to me in class as a reference on the job. | |

| THE INSTRUCTOR | RATING |
|---|---|
| 1. Presented the materials clearly. | |
| 2. Explained how each activity related to the overall objective. | |
| 3. Encouraged class participation. | |

| OVERALL | RATING |
|---|---|
| 1. The discussion topic accomplished the stated objectives. | |
| 2. This program was worth the time spent away from my job. | |

Softlines Merchandising, Food Financial Management, General Managers' Command and Communication, and Fundamentals of Supervision.

Level 1 evaluations will be conducted in a two-step process for 100 percent of the classes taught by Corporate University. The first step involves a pencil-and-paper assessment that will be passed out to associates during the training session (see Exhibit 3.11). This evaluation provides an instructor with immediate feedback on the course material presented and the associates' facilitation skills. The second step uses the web portal and has been designed to collect associates' reactions to the class after having had up to a week to reflect on the training. This evaluation is similar to the one given in the classroom. The instructor is asked to direct the associate to an URL that will allow access to the online assessment both during the class and in a postclass e-mail. We anticipated a drop in the response rate but have seen the quality of responses improve significantly in the classes that have been taught early in the training calendar. This improvement can be attributed to the associate having time to analyze and reflect back on the information provided in the class and not having to rush to complete the level 1 "smile sheet." The educational support team will review the feedback and provide an analysis to the instructors and their supervisors for review.

All of the examples we have described above are comment sheets (or "smile sheets," as some people call them) to be completed by the participants immediately after the course or online to measure Reaction. Another source of the reaction of learners can come from focus groups, described below.

## Focus Groups

Jim was working with the Canada Revenue Agency on how to enhance the evaluation of their Employee Orientation Program for New Managers. As part of his recommendations, he suggested a standard, targeted level 1 Reaction sheet to be administered immediately after each course. This tool contained questions about content, facilities, trainers, food, and instructional methods.

Leaders of the group asked Jim, "Why don't you include questions on relevance? It is very important that these trainees tell us to what degree the concepts, principles, and techniques that we are teaching are relevant to their jobs." In this particular case, Jim had a specific answer: "How do they know? They have not been managers yet, and they will not be able to give you any kind of an answer or helpful information until they have been on the job for a month or more. So, don't ask them until then."

The following case study describes how a Reaction sheet and focus groups were used.

------------

# Evaluating an Orientation Program for New Managers

Canada Revenue Agency, Pacific Division
David Barron, Regional Learning and Development Advisor
Vancouver, British Columbia

This orientation training program was called Jump Start to Management. It was designed to be sure that new managers got off to the right start. The leaders of the program used both a survey and a questionnaire to obtain level 1 information.

Jim suggested that they use a focus group to measure level 2 learning, by inviting a mixed group of eight to ten graduates to sit and dialogue with a trained facilitator for about one and one-half hours. Here is the approach using some of the questions from the Reaction sheet.

The group was told,

> It has been three months since you attended the Jump Start to Management training program. You have had a good chance to work in a new job, so we thought it would be a good idea to get some of your thoughts so that we can improve future programs.

The first question they were asked was "Why did you attend the session?"

After considering their answers, the leader reviewed the program and discussed each module, one at a time. The leader then asked the following questions:

1. What was most helpful about the module?
2. How helpful were the activities?
3. What was not helpful?
4. What specific elements of the program had the most positive impact on you? Why?

5. What suggestions do you have for improving the program?
6. What specific successes have you had in applying different elements of the program?
7. What challenges have you faced, or what factors have discouraged or kept you from applying them?
8. What results have you seen from your efforts so far?

Focus groups reach beyond level 1 into levels 2 and 3 and even sneak into level 4.

The first question was a general motivation question.

Questions 1–5 concern levels 1 and 2. Questions 6 and 7 are about level 3, applying learning to the job. And the last question delves into level 4.

We call this approach a "combination tool." In this case, there are a number of purposes.

First, it elicits information from participants that would not be available immediately after the program. Second, it demonstrates to the participants that someone cares about their experiences on their new jobs. Third, it shows participants that the three-day program was not just some time away from work. Instead, it was to teach them new knowledge and skills in order to perform their jobs effectively and make a positive contribution to their direct reports and to the organization. That is a mouthful, but it represents an additional benefit of effective evaluation at no extra charge!

By the way, Jim also recommends that a very powerful question, one that is not typically asked, be added to the initial level 1 Reaction sheet:

How well do you understand what you learned and how will you apply what you learned on the job?

The answers you get can be very telling!

## Summary

You may call them comment sheets, Reaction sheets, smile sheets, or happiness sheets, but be sure you have the right items to evaluate in order to measure Reaction. Consider the guidelines we have described, and end the form with the question "What would have improved the program?"

Keep in mind the two reasons for doing it.

First of all, they are your *customers*, whether they pay or not. And you better send them away from the program or the computer "satisfied." Some peers, bosses, and/or future participants will probably ask the participants, "What did you think of the training program you took?" And we think you can guess the possible ramifications of them saying such things as "It was a waste of time," "I sure didn't learn anything that will help me do my job better," or "Don't waste your time taking it unless you have to."

Yes, there is a good chance that the word will get to someone in upper management who will not bother to get overall reactions to the program, but will draw some bad conclusions about the training department and make some decisions accordingly. So get their reactions and be sure they are positive by considering the Ten Requirements for an Effective Training Program described in Chapter 1.

And, then, there is a second reason for using Reaction sheets. If you don't use them, the trainees may feel that you are tactfully telling them that you know what they need and you don't need any input from them to tell you how effective the program was. And they may not like that.

Evaluate reactions on *every program* even though you think you know what their reactions will be. If you are teaching a class, it is easy to get a 100 percent response. If you are doing e-learning, do your best to get as great a response as possible. Make it easy for them to reply, keep it short and simple, and encourage promptness.

The guidelines we have provided should be helpful. And don't forget to look at all the forms included in this chapter. And don't hesitate to "borrow" and/or adapt those that you want to use in evaluating Reaction to your programs.

# Chapter 4

# Implementing Level 2: Learning

Evaluating level 1, Reaction, is important for two reasons. First, the participants are your customers and you need to know how they feel about the program they have attended or taken online. They had better be "satisfied" or you are in trouble. The second reason is the feeling they might get if you didn't ask for their reaction. It would probably indicate to some that you know how they feel or don't care.

Being "satisfied" doesn't necessarily mean that they learned anything. They may have based their reaction on their enjoyment of the course. In the presentations we make and in the workshops we conduct, we are frequently told by participants, "I really enjoyed the program," and they say it with enthusiasm. We then ask them, "How about the P?" This refers to the "P" in PIE, our approach to teaching. The "P" stands for Practical, while the "I" refers to Interactive, and the "E" for Enjoyable. We see no problem in having a program that is enjoyable if the P comes first.

In any training program, there are three possible objectives:

- For the participants to acquire *knowledge* related to their jobs
- For participants to learn new *skills* and/or increase their present skills
- For participants to change their *attitudes*

It is important to measure learning because no change in behavior can be expected unless one or more of these learning objectives have been accomplished. Moreover, if you were to measure behavior change (level 3) and not learning and if you found no change in behavior, the likely conclusion would be that no learning took place. This conclusion may be very erroneous. The reason no change in behavior was observed may be that the climate was preventing or discouraging it. In these situations, learning may have taken place, and the learner may even have been anxious to change his or her behavior. But because his or her boss either prevented or discouraged the trainee from applying his or her learning on the job, no change in behavior took place.

The measurement of learning is more difficult and time-consuming than the measurement of reaction. These guidelines will be helpful.

## Guidelines for Evaluating Learning

1. Use a control group if practical.
2. Evaluate knowledge, skills, and/or attitudes both before and after the program.
   a. Use a "paper-and-pencil" or online test to measure changes in knowledge and attitudes.
   b. Use a performance test to measure increase in skills.
3. Get a 100 percent response, if possible.
4. Use the evaluation results to take appropriate action.

The remainder of this chapter suggests ways of implementing these guidelines.

## Use a Control Group if Practical

The best way to "prove" that learning took place in a training program is to compare the results of tests from an "experimental" group that received the training with those of a "control" group that did not receive the training. There is a slight problem in doing this. Unless both groups are alike in all significant factors such as job duties, education, background experience, age, attitudes, and so on, the comparison is not valid.

Therefore, unless you are from an organization that is large enough and has experts on selecting control and experimental groups, forget it. And even if they were "exactly" alike, there is a problem when those attending the program have contact with those who don't and pass on information or skills they learned. So the words "if practical" are very important for most organizations to consider.

## Use "Paper-and-Pencil" or Online Tests

These tests should be used to measure increase in knowledge and changes in attitudes. Administer a pretest (the test given prior to starting the program) and posttest (the same test given after the program) if the participants might have previous knowledge of the subject. Obviously, if the program content is all new, only a posttest would be used.

In designing the test, here are factors to consider:

1. The test must cover the content of the program and the knowledge, skills, and/or attitudes to be learned. Standardized tests may be found that meet this requirement. If not, the test must be specifically designed for the program.
2. The length of the test should be reasonable in relation to the length and content of the program.
3. Use any one or combination of the following test items:
   • Agree or disagree
   • True or false
   • Multiple choice
   • Sentence completion
   • Matching
   The use of "Agree" and "Disagree" and of "True" and "False" allows participants to guess right and perhaps make the test less valid than the other three choices.
4. Target the test language to the audience.

We are going to describe some of the approaches we have used. Then, we will quote from the approaches used in the various case studies in the book *Evaluating Training Programs: The Four Levels*, third edition.

If increased knowledge and/or changed attitudes are being measured, an online or "paper-and-pencil" test can be used. (This term must have been coined before ballpoint pens were invented.)

There are two practical ways of doing this. One way is to determine the knowledge, skills, and attitudes that a supervisor should have, and develop the subject content accordingly. Then develop a test that measures the knowledge, skills, and attitudes, and give it to participants as a pretest. If the pretest is administered in advance of the program, an analysis of the results will provide information to use in determining subject content.

The other approach is to purchase a standardized instrument that relates closely to the subject matter being taught. The sixty-five-item Management Inventory on Managing Change (MIMC) is an example of a standardized test. I (Don) use it when teaching a supervisory workshop on Managing Change, primarily to stimulate discussion. It could also be used on a pretest and posttest basis to measure increase in knowledge.

Following are ten items from it. The "correct" answers were determined by me to cover the concepts, principles, and techniques for managing change that I taught.

Instructions: Please circle the A if you agree and the D if you disagree.

A    D    1. If subordinates participate in the decision to make a change, they are usually more enthusiastic in carrying it out.

A    D    2. Some people are not anxious to be promoted to a job that has more responsibility.

A    D    3. Decisions to change should be based on opinions as well as on facts.

A    D    4. If a change is going to be unpopular with your subordinates, you should proceed slowly in order to obtain acceptance.

A    D    5. It is usually better to communicate with a group concerning a change than to talk to its members individually.

A    D    6. Empathy is one of the most important concepts in managing change.

A    D    7. It's a good idea to sell a change to the natural leader before trying to sell it to the others.

A    D    8. If you are promoted to a management job, you should make the job different from what it was under your predecessor.

A   D    9. Bosses and subordinates should have an understanding regarding the kinds of changes that the subordinate can implement without getting prior approval from the boss.

A   D   10. You should encourage your subordinates to try out any changes that they feel should be made.

Example 1 in Table 4.1 illustrates the use of experimental and control groups to measure learning of knowledge. It shows that the average score of the experimental group on the pretest was 45.5 on a possible score of 65. The average score of the experimental group on the posttest was 55.4, a net gain of 9.9.

Example 1 also shows that the average score of the control group on the pretest was 46.7 and that of the control group on the posttest was 48.2, a gain of 1.5. This means that factors other than the training program caused the change. Therefore, the gain of 1.5 of the control group must be deducted from the 9.9 gain of the experimental group to show the gain resulting from the training program. The result is 8.4.

Example 2 in Table 4.1 shows a different story. The net gain for the control group between the pretest score of 46.7 and the posttest score of 54.4 is 7.7. When this difference is deducted from the 9.9 regis-

Table 4.1. Pretest and Posttest Scores
on the Management Inventory on Managing Change

|  |  | Experimental group | Control group |
|---|---|---|---|
| Example 1 | Pretest | 45.5 | 46.7 |
|  | Posttest | 55.4 | 48.2 |
|  | Gain | +9.9 | +1.5 |
|  |  | Net Gain 9.9 − 1.5 = 8.4 | |
|  |  | Experimental group | Control group |
| Example 2 | Pretest | 45.5 | 46.7 |
|  | Posttest | 55.4 | 54.4 |
|  | Gain | +9.9 | +7.7 |
|  |  | Net Gain 9.9 − 7.7 = 2.2 | |

tered for the experimental group, the gain that can be attributed to the training program is only 2.2.

The comparison of total scores on the pretest and posttest is one method of measuring increased knowledge and/or changes in attitude.

Another important measure involves the comparison of pretest and posttest answers to each item on the inventory or test. For example, item 4 of the MIMC states, "If a change is going to be unpopular with your subordinates, you should proceed slowly in order to obtain acceptance."

Table 4.2 shows that seven of the twenty-five supervisors in the experimental group agreed with item 4 on the pretest, and eighteen disagreed. It also shows that twenty agreed with it on the posttest, and five disagreed. The correct answer is "Agree," so the positive gain was 13. Table 4.2 also shows the pretest and posttest responses from the

Table 4.2. Responses to Two Items
on the Management Inventory on Managing Change

Item 4.  "If a change is going to be unpopular with your subordinates, you should proceed slowly in order to obtain acceptance." (The correct answer is *Agree*.)

|  | Experimental group | | Control group | |
|---|---|---|---|---|
|  | *Agree* | *Disagree* | *Agree* | *Disagree* |
| Pretest | 7 | 18 | 6 | 19 |
| Posttest | 20 | 5 | 7 | 18 |
| Gain | +13 | | +1 | |
|  | | Net Gain 13 − 1 = 12 | | |

Item 8.  "If you are promoted to a management job, you should make the job different than it was under your predecessor." (The correct answer is *Agree*.)

|  | Experimental group | | Control group | |
|---|---|---|---|---|
|  | *Agree* | *Disagree* | *Agree* | *Disagree* |
| Pretest | 5 | 20 | 5 | 20 |
| Posttest | 6 | 19 | 6 | 19 |
| Gain | +1 | | +1 | |
|  | | Net Gain 1 − 1 = 0 | | |

control group. For item 4, the gain was 1. Therefore, the net gain due to the training program was 12.

Item 8 in Table 4.2 shows a different story. Item 8 states, "If you are promoted to a management job, you should make the job different than it was under your predecessor."

Five of those in the experimental group agreed on the pretest, and twenty disagreed. On the posttest, six agreed, and nineteen disagreed. The correct answer is "Agree." The net gain was 1. The figures for the control group were the same. So there was no change in attitude and/or knowledge on this item.

This approach to the evaluation of learning is important for two reasons. First, the measurement of the increase in correct total scores shows how effective the trainer was in accomplishing the objectives of the session. It would be easy to blame the learners for not learning because of various factors, but, if the objective is to teach the learners certain concepts, principles, and techniques, the instructor should look at him or herself and ask, "Why didn't they learn, and what can I do next time to improve learning?" Just as important is the specific information that evaluation of learning provides. By analyzing the change in answers to individual items, the instructor can see where he or she has succeeded and where he or she has failed to accomplish the objectives of the session. If the program is going to be repeated, the instructor can plan other techniques and/or aids to increase the chances that learning will take place on the items where little or no change took place in previous sessions. Moreover, if follow-up sessions can be held with the same group, the things that have not been learned can become the objectives of these sessions.

These examples have illustrated how a control group can be used to compare with the experimental group. In most organizations, it is not practical to have a control group, and the evaluation will include only figures for those who attended the training program. The question then becomes, "How satisfied are you with the results of the increase in total scores and the changes in response to each item?"

We have two possible answers. If you can find a statistician in your organization who will help (check with Human Resources), then the answers to the effectiveness can be analyzed statistically to determine the significance of the changes. If you cannot find such a person, then use your own judgment and decide how satisfied you are with the results.

It almost goes without saying that a standardized test can be used only to the extent that it covers the subject matter taught in the training program. When I (Don) teach, I use the various inventories that I have developed as teaching tools. Each inventory includes much of the content of the corresponding program. The same principles and techniques can and should be used with a test developed specifically for the organization.

For example, MGIC, a mortgage insurer in Milwaukee, has developed an extensive test covering information that its supervisors need to know. Much of this information is related to the specific policies, procedures, and facts of the business and organization.

The trainers then wrote a test covering that information. They combined true-or-false statements with multiple-choice items and administered the test prior to the training program. A tabulation of the pretest responses to each item will tell the instructors what the supervisors do and do not know before they participate in the program. This will help the instructors determine the specific needs of the participants and decide what items require the most attention.

If everyone knows the answer to an item before the program takes place, there may be little or no need to cover that item in the program.

A tabulation of posttest responses will tell the instructors where they have succeeded or failed in getting the participants to learn the information that the test covers. It will help instructors know what they need to emphasize and whether they need to use more aids in future programs. It will also tell them what follow-up programs are needed.

This type of test is different from the inventories described earlier. Participants must know the answers to the questions in Exhibit 4.1. Therefore, those who take the posttest must put their names on it, and they are graded. Those who do not pass must take further training until they pass the test.

In regard to the inventories, there is no need to identify the responses and scores of individual persons. The scoring sheet shown in Exhibit 4.2 is given to participants. They score their own inventory and circle the number of each item that they answered incorrectly. They keep their inventory and turn in the scoring sheet. These can be tabulated to determine both the total scores and the responses to individual items. You can then use the results as shown in Tables 4.1 and 4.2 in planning future programs.

The MIMC and the MGIC examples are typical of efforts to measure increase in knowledge and/or changes in attitudes.

As an example of another approach, in a weeklong program I (Don) conducted for twenty-five executives at ServiceMaster in

Exhibit 4.1. Sample Items from a MGIC Test to Evaluate Supervisor Knowledge

---

1. T or F     When preparing a truth-in-lending disclosure with a financed single premium, mortgage insurance should always be disclosed for the life of the loan.

2. T or F     GE and MGIC have the same refund policy for refundable single premiums.

3. T or F     MGIC, GE, and PMI are the only mortgage insurers offering a non-refundable single premium.

4. _____      Which of the following is not a category in the loan progress reports?

     a. Loans approved

     b. Loans-in-suspense

     c. Loans denied

     d. Loans received

5. _____      Which of the following do not affect the MGIC Plus buying decision?

     a. Consumer

     b. Realtor

     c. MGIC underwriter

     d. Secondary market manager

     e. Servicing manager

     f. All the above

     g. None of the above

     h. Both b and c

     i. Both c and e

6. _____      The new risk-based capital regulations for savings and loans have caused many of them to

     a. Convert whole loans into securities

     b. Begin originating home equity loans

     c. Put MI on their uninsured 90s

     d. All the above

     e. Both e and c

     f. Both b and c

---

Exhibit 4.2. Scoring Sheet for the Management Inventory on Managing Change

---

*Management Inventory on Managing Change*          Date _____

Please circle by number those items you answered incorrectly according to the scoring key. Then determine your score by subtracting the number wrong from 65.

| 1 | 2 | 3 | 4 | 5 | 6 | 7 | 8 | 9 | 10 | 11 | 12 | 13 | 14 | 15 | 16 | 17 | 18 |
|---|---|---|---|---|---|---|---|---|----|----|----|----|----|----|----|----|----|
| 19 | 20 | 21 | 22 | 23 | 24 | 25 | 26 | 27 | 28 | 29 | 30 | 31 | 32 | 33 | 34 |
| 35 | 36 | 37 | 38 | 39 | 40 | 41 | 42 | 43 | 44 | 45 | 46 | 47 | 48 | 49 | 50 |
| 51 | 52 | 53 | 54 | 55 | 56 | 57 | 58 | 59 | 60 | 61 | 62 | 63 | 64 | 65 |

Score   65 –        =

---

Downers Grove, Illinois, I used a matching questionnaire to measure learning.

In this program on leadership, I used twenty-five matches, including the following:

_____ 1. Hierarchy of needs          A. Blake and Mouton
_____ 2. Johari window               B. McGregor
_____ 3. Quality vs. acceptance      C. Churchill
_____ 4. Theory "X" and theory "Y"   D. Ted
_____ 5. The managerial grid         E. Joe and Harry
_____ 6. "Give us the tools and
            we'll finish the job"       F. Maslow
_____ 7. I'll spin                   G. Maier

You probably noticed that some of them seem to have little to do with leadership and others may have been popular prior to your training experience. The point is that you can use the matching approach to measure participants' learning on any program, no matter what the content.

If you get number 7 correct, it is strictly by a process of elimination.

I told the group about my son Ted being on *Wheel of Fortune*. In fact, I showed them a clip of part of the show. It was on my wife's birthday, and she and I were watching it on TV. He had discovered the puzzle early in the round. But he is a risk taker and wanted to get all the possible money by continuing to guess the letters. The only danger was to get "Lose a Turn" or "Bankrupt." Well, he kept saying, "I'll

Exhibit 4.3. Decision-Making

| | Manager | | | |
|---|---|---|---|---|
| *QUALITY* | *Subordinates* | | *ACCEPTANCE* | |
| | *Past* | | *Future* | |
| | *Average (%)* | *Range (%)* | *Average (%)* | *Range (%)* |
| 1. Manager decides and sells decision. | 25 | 10–50 | 16 | 5–40 |
| 2. Manager asks for input, considers it, decides, and sells decision. | 37 | 10–50 | 30 | 10–50 |
| 3. Manager leads subordinates to a consensus decision. | 22 | 10–50 | 25 | 5–50 |
| 4. Manager empowers subordinates to make the decision. | 16 | 0–40 | 29 | 0–60 |
| Total | 100 | | 100 | |

*Note*: *N*=25 ServiceMaster executives.

spin" until he had got to $3,300 with one more letter to guess, which he knew, of course. I yelled into the TV, "*Take the money!*" but he said, "*I'll spin one more time.*" Guess what?

Some of you guessed right, and some wrong. The arrow stopped in the center of $5,000! Pat Sajak said, "You rascal!"

P.S. If you want to know the correct answers to the matches, and/or what he picked as a prize, please e-mail Don.

At ServiceMaster, I (Don) used a different approach to illustrate a change in attitudes. (This is the same example I used at the beginning of Chapter 2.)

I (Don) learned from Norman Maier (used in the matching exercise) to present two aspects of decision-making: the quality of the decision and the acceptance by those affected by the decision. I presented the four ways that managers can use to make decisions, which are illustrated in Exhibit 4.3.

I then asked the twenty-five ServiceMaster executives what percentage of times they have used the four choices in the past. I then presented two concepts:

1. That they might get good or bad decisions using any of the four
2. That the level of acceptance increases as the level of participation increases

In the first choice, there is no participation.

In the second there is some, depending of course on whether the manager listens to employees and considers their input in making the decision.

In the third choice, problem solving, those affected come to a consensus with the manager as facilitator, who is careful not to influence the group.

In the fourth choice, empowerment, the group makes the decision independent of the manager, and the manager agrees to implement it. This illustrates "complete ownership."

It becomes obvious that the level of acceptance is related to the amount of participation. As George Odiorne stated in his book *The Change Masters*, "If you want others to accept your decisions, give them a feeling of 'ownership'!"

My objective was to get them to change their attitude toward decision-making and agree to increase the amount of participation when making decisions because of the acceptance factor. Did I succeed?

Exhibit 4.3 shows that the average for each of their past choices was 25 percent for number 1, 37 percent for number 2, 22 percent for number 3, and 16 percent for number 4. Their choices in making future decisions were 16 percent for number 1, 30 percent for number 2, 25 percent for number 3, and 29 percent for number 4. These are very significant changes.

This shows that they learned the importance of acceptance when making decisions and that they plan to use more participation in the future. An interesting item is that one person said 0 percent for using number 4, empowerment. The reason is probably because the subordinates are not qualified to make decisions because they are new and do not know enough about the decision, or because the risk is too great to leave it entirely up to them.

This example demonstrates a change in attitudes. When the executives get back to the job, the question becomes a matter of level 3, "Will the Learning transfer to Behavior?" This will be discussed in the next chapter.

One final note about knowledge and attitude tests. Certain individuals, groups, and even organizations do not like the word "test." They believe it intimidates the participants and creates a negative feeling. They have found several ways to address that. First, some of them administer tests and call them "quizzes." (We are not sure they are fooling anyone, however.)

Others provide for "knowledge checks." These consist of a list of key concepts, principles, and/or techniques from a program. They administer it some time after the course by having each course participant meet with either an experienced peer or supervisor and talk through the list, telling the other what they know about it. While this does not provide the rigor that an objective test does, it oftentimes meets the needs of a less formal evaluation. Others rely on formative evaluation during the course. Level 2 evaluation checks are woven into the curriculum so that the instructor of the course and/or peers check knowledge and attitudes along the way. However, a final posttest is probably needed to compare with the pretest to measure learning for the entire program.

## Use Performance Tests to Measure Skills

If the objective of a program is to increase the skills of participants, then a performance test is needed. For example, some programs aim at improving presentation skills. A trained instructor can evaluate the level of proficiency by using a checklist of the various ingredients of effective presentations. Other trainers may also be qualified if they have been given standards of performance. For the pretest, each person can give a short talk before any training has been given. The instructor can measure these talks and assign them a grade on each aspect of presenting. During the program, the instructor provides principles and techniques for making an effective talk. The increase in skills can be measured for each succeeding talk that participants give by comparing pretraining scores with posttraining scores. The same approach can be used to measure such skills as writing, conducting meetings, conducting performance appraisal interviews, using a computer, making out forms, and selling. An evaluation of the skill after instruction measures the learning that has taken place.

Obviously, as mentioned before, there should be no pretest if the information is new and none of the participants know it.

In order to measure learning, anything less than a response from all participants requires a carefully designed approach to select a sample group and analyze the results statistically. (Here is the need for that statistician again.) But, it is usually not difficult to get everyone in the group to participate, and tabulations become quite simple.

Tables 4.1 and 4.2 show how this can be done.

The rest of the chapter will consist of tests and other approaches illustrated in the following case studies from *Evaluating Training Programs: The Four Levels*, third edition.

---

## Evaluating a Leadership Training Program

### Gap Inc.
### Don Kraft, Manager, Corporate Training
### San Bruno, California

In the Gap case study, participant learning was evaluated using the Leadership Training for Supervisors (LTS) Questionnaire. The LTS Questionnaire is a fill-in-the-blank test with fifty-five possible answers. See Exhibit 4.4.

A sample of 17 percent of total participants completed the questionnaire at the end of the LTS program. The questionnaire was completed anonymously. While completing the questionnaire, participants were not permitted to use any notes or program materials. Results were then tabulated by division.

The facilitators who delivered the program received detailed written and oral instructions on how to administer the questionnaire. Participants were told on the first day of the training that a questionnaire would be administered to determine the effectiveness of the LTS program.

The LTS Questionnaire was scored on a percentage basis by the number of correct answers. Each blank was equal to one point. All questionnaires were scored by Gap Inc. Corporate Training Department.

In the case study of the Army and Air Force Exchange Service (AAFES), described in Chapter 3, level 2 evaluations were conducted for 80 percent of the courses taught. These assessments were given by the instructor on a pretest and posttest basis. (See Exhibit 4.5.) In order for associates to receive course credit in their personnel records,

### Exhibit 4.4. LTS Questionnaire

---

Check your division:    Gap _____     GapKids _____     Banana Republic _____

UK _____     Canada _____

Check your manager level:   District manager _____    Store manager _____

General manager _____    Area manager _____

Complete the following questions by filling in the blanks.

1. What are the three skills that situational leaders use when working to develop people to eventually manage themselves?

    1. _____

    2. _____

    3. _____

2. A person at D2 (Disillusioned Learner) has _____ competence and _____ commitment.

3. Diagnose the development level of the individual in this situation.

Eric has begun working on a merchandising project that is important to his store. He has successfully completed previous merchandising projects in the past but feels there is some pressure on him. He is already involved in other projects and is beginning to feel discouraged because of the time crunch.

Eric's development level on this project is _____ .

4. Competence is a measure of a person's _____ and _____ related to the task or goal at hand.

5. Describe what a style 4 leader (Delegating) does. List three behaviors/actions you would see a style 4 leader take.

    1. _____

    2. _____

    3. _____

6. A person at D4 (Peak Performer) has _____ competence and _____ commitment.

7. In order to listen well, a supervisor must concentrate. What are two examples of concentration techniques?

    1. _____

    2. _____

8. Commitment is a measure of a person's _____ and _____ with regard to the task or goal at hand.

9. Describe what a style 2 leader (Coaching) does. List three behaviors/actions you would see a style 2 leader take.

    1. _____

    2. _____

    3. _____

*(continued)*

Exhibit 4.4. LTS Questionnaire (*continued*)

---

10. Define "leadership."

11. Who takes the lead in goal setting, feedback, decision-making, and problem solving in leadership styles 1 and 2?

12. A person at D1 (Enthusiastic Beginner) has _____ competence and _____ commitment.

13. Define the acronym for a SMART goal.

    S _____

    M _____

    A _____

    R _____

    T _____

14. When contracting, whose perception should prevail if a supervisor and employee do not agree on the same development level?

15. Describe what a style 3 leader (Supporting) does. List three behaviors/actions you would see a style 3 leader take.

    1. _____

    2. _____

    3. _____

16. To create a positive interaction with an employee, a supervisor's attention must be focused on _____ and _____ .

17. List four examples of what you see someone doing or hear someone saying to be a good listener.

    1. _____

    2. _____

    3. _____

    4. _____

18. When monitoring performance, supervisors reinforce performance standards by using three methods of giving feedback. They are _____ , _____ , and _____ .

19. Suppose you have a sales associate, Becky, who needs to improve her listening skills. Create a goal for improving Becky's listening skills using the formula for a clear goal.

20. Encouraging dialogue means using attentive body language. What are two examples of body language?

    1. _____

    2. _____

Exhibit 4.4. LTS Questionnaire (*continued*)

---

21. Interactions a supervisor has with an employee that have a positive or negative impact on that person's performance and satisfaction are called
_____ .

22. A person at D3 (Emerging Contributor) has _____ and _____ commitment.

23. Describe what a style 1 leader (Directing) does. List three behaviors/actions you would see a style 1 leader take.
    1. _____
    2. _____
    3. _____

24. When communicating, a sender sends a message three ways:
    1. _____
    2. _____
    3. _____

25. Who takes the lead in goal setting, feedback, decision-making, and problem solving in leadership styles 3 and 4?

---

they had to pass the posttest with a score of 80 percent or higher. Instructors compared the results from pretests and posttests to evaluate the questions and see if any patterns existed that require the adjustment of future training or the modification of test questions. The tests were developed by the course designers to ensure that the course objectives have been met during the training session.

Exhibit 4.5. Measuring Learning

---

1. **Associates showing expensive items to a customer should show no more than this many at one time:**
   a. 1          b. 2          c. 3          d. 4

2. **Greeters should do their best to completely secure the shopping bags of customers entering the store:**
   a. True          b. False

3. **Cameras should be considered for small stores who have concerns about physical security.**
   a. True          b. False

(*continued*)

Exhibit 4.5. Measuring Learning (*continued*)

---

4. **While associates are checking for concealed merchandise at register, they should detain any customer concealing items.**

    a. True        b. False

5. **In-store quarterly refresher loss prevention training should include:**

    a. Intranet tutorials                               c. Topic in store meetings
    b. Safety & Security personnel assisted training    d. All of these choices

6. **Define a "detention":**

    _____
    _____
    _____

7. **A store's unobserved losses are typically only _____ % of the actual losses.**

8. **When it comes to physical security, which of the following is the most important physical condition:**

    a. Trimmed shrubs and bushes            c. Having a good peep hole
    b. Locating trash cans near the exit door   d. Good lighting

9. **What is the percentage of robberies that occur just before or after closing?**

    a. 33%          b. 25%          c. 50%          d. 75%

10. **This person must approve any one-person closing operation:**

    a. Store Manager  b. General Manager   c. Region Vice President

11. **Do your best to estimate the amount of loss after a robbery and inform the authorities.**

    a. True        b. False

12. **ARFIS automatically tracks customers who:**
    a. don't have ID cards    b. don't have receipts    c. make frequent purchases.

13. **Monthly, what % of refund customers should be called (with or without receipt)?**

    a. 5%            c. 15%            e. None of these choices

    b. 10%           d. 20%

14. **There is not presently a tutorial available for shoplifting prevention, but one is coming soon.**

    a. True        b. False

15. **One should avoid conducting training only with the associate that has not appropriately followed an internal control as it occurs. This would make sure more of your staff was trained together at a future point in time.**

    a. True        b. False

Exhibit 4.5. Measuring Learning (*continued*)

---

16. **This is the #1 organizational characteristic that contributes to employee dishonesty:**

17. **List two acceptable reasons for a price override:**

18. **You should assign an associate to prepare a price change voucher for the total listed on the price difference report each week.**
    a. True          b. False

19. **When providing a customer an adjustment for a price discrepancy or a sales promotion 30-day guarantee, the adjustment key under refunds on the cash register will take care of your accountability.**
    a. True          b. False

20. **Name three ways the store capture rate may be improved:**

21. **When an item doesn't capture, adding it to ASAP will fix this problem.**
    a. True          b. False

22. **A customer laptop awaiting repair is not considered critical while in your store.**
    a. True          b. False

23. **This report is used to determine what did not capture daily:**
    a. Daily Sales Error Report          d. SD RPOS Sub department Rings Report
    b. Price Difference Report
    c. Tlog Report

24. **An item that shows E and F in ASAP under item inquiry does not capture.**
    a. True          b. False

25. **When creating local promotions in the ISP, use the file that starts with this number to ensure markdowns are being booked to the SPS:**
    a. 1          b. 2          c. 3          d. 4

26. **You should control the following people in your store:** (*circle all that apply*)
    a. Vendors     b. Military inspectors          c. General Manager

(*continued*)

Exhibit 4.5. Measuring Learning (*continued*)

---

27. **Transaction voids may be made occasionally a few transactions after the voided transaction, when the void has nothing to do with customer service.**

    a. True          b. False

28. **Under what circumstance is refund approval required for an AAFES employee?**

    _____

29. **Security tape should be available at each cash register in your store.**

    a. True          b. False

30. **List one good reason for a department ring, other than equipment failure:**

    _____

31. **List three significant potentially negative outcomes of using departmental rings:**

    a. _____
    b. _____
    c. _____

32. **What categories of merchandise are required to be treated as Critical?**

    a. _____
    b. _____
    c. _____

---

# Evaluating Training for an Outage Management System

## PacifiCorp
### Dan Schuch, PowerLearning Training Developer
### Portland, Oregon

In the case study of PacifiCorp, another practical way of measuring the learning of knowledge and skills was to have the learners perform in the classroom and be judged accordingly. (See Exhibit 4.6.)

PowerLearning was the name of a training branch of PacifiCorp. Here are the details of their approach to measuring learning.

Exhibit 4.6. Measuring Learning

The level 2 assessment for this training of a new computer system was given as a competency check list. The questions carefully matched the objectives of the course. Each person taking the class was required to demonstrate competency to the instructor on each specific task listed. Various factors required this training to be conducted one on one. This task list was given out to all the learners even prior to the training, and a blank assessment was provided to all learners after completion. Distributing the checklist before the training provides the person with the important elements of the training before it starts. The learner can also use this checklist to supplement the training to help verify abilities after the training. A section of this assessment is provided here.

WS500 Navigation—Performance Assessment

The student will achieve the goal of the course by completing the presented objectives. These objectives are achieved by demonstrating competency to the instructor in the specific behaviors assigned to each objective. Students must demonstrate mastery in each objective to earn credit for this course.

| Procedure<br>*To accomplish . . .* | Objectives<br>*Demonstrate the<br>ability to . . .* | Tasks<br>*By showing you can . . .* | Demonstrated |
|---|---|---|---|
| Logging into the system | Log In | Launch WS500 from desktop | |
| | Shift Change Log In | Log in while another operator is already logged in | |
| | Log Out | Log out of the WS500 | |
| | Change Password | Change the WS500 password | |
| Working with Displays | Open Displays Using the File Method | Open the master menu (MSTRMENU) in a new window using the filter and wildcard characters | |
| | | Open a substation index display in the same window from a poke point on the Master Menu | |

*(continued)*

67

Exhibit 4.6. Measuring Learning (*continued*)

| Procedure<br>*To accomplish . . .* | Objectives<br>*Demonstrate the<br>ability to . . . .* | Tasks<br>*By showing you can . . .* | Demonstrated |
|---|---|---|---|
| Working with<br>Displays (*cont.*) | Open Displays Using the<br>File Method (*cont.*) | Open a substation one-line display in a new window from a poke<br>point on the substation index display | |
| | Navigate Between<br>Displays | Navigate to a display previously open in the active window using<br>Display Recall buttons | |
| | | View the display history for the window using Display Recall<br>and select a display to open | |
| | | Navigate to another open display using the Window drop down<br>menu | |

In addition to being able to measure the effects of our training better, we have received a number of additional benefits as a result of implementing level 2 assessments in our training programs. We found that the level 2 assessment could also serve as a teaching tool. The answers to the assessment were reviewed with the class upon completion of the assessment. We were delighted to discover that in a couple of instances, material covered during the course was clarified. We noted that students would pose additional questions that were answered by both the instructors and other classmates and led to a richer training experience.

The level 2 assessment provided a content check for the instructors. In one specific instance, it was identified during the debrief time that an important point covered in the assessment was not covered in the depth that it needed to be addressed during the training. A potential problem was averted by reviewing the assessment after the class. The assessment provided a valuable and time-saving check on the training.

The use of the level 2 assessments also improved the consistency of content presented by the different trainers, because we found that having the different instructors use the same level 2 assessment for a given course as a benchmark has helped us to bridge the gaps in training and learning outcomes between instructors. Differences are quickly identified and resolved before the actual training begins.

The implementation of level 2 assessments has gone smoothly, and there has been complete support from the class participants for the courses we have developed. Instructors and class participants have a better idea of what is important in the class, and the level 2 evaluations enforce consistency between the instructional content and the course objectives. Development of the level 2 assessment has helped focus the training development. Extraneous material is removed from the instruction, and objectives are added and refined to better match important instructional material. This has helped streamline our courses to include only the relevant and important content.

An additional benefit is that the level 2 assessment is also being used as a teaching tool. The level 2 assessment can help validate learners' understanding and increase instructors' confidence that the class participants have mastered the material covered in the class. In situations when a student is not able to demonstrate competency, instructors are provided with a good opportunity to clarify and answer questions.

The following case study from Spain provides a different approach.

## Evaluating a Coaching and Counseling Course

Group Iberdrola
Gema Gongora, Training and Development Manager
Consultants
Epise, Barcelona
Juan Pablo Ventosa, Managing Director
Nuria Duran, Project Manager
Madrid, Spain

Because the educational goals of the course included not only knowledge but skills as well, the consulting firm that gave the course was asked to conduct one test of knowledge and another of skills. For this purpose, the firm designed questionnaires and guidelines for observation. These can be seen in Exhibits 4.7 and 4.8.

The participants took the knowledge test at the beginning and end of the training event. The trainer applied the observation guidelines to the role-playing activities that took place during the course.

## Evaluating a Career Development Initiative

Innovative Computer, Inc.
Holly Burkett, M.A., SPHR, CPT
Principal, Evaluation Works
Davis, California

In this case study, the skill and knowledge gaps were first determined. From these, specific learning needs were determined that were reflected in the level 2 learning objectives for the program. Specifically, as shown in the data collection plan, participants identified skills, talents, and development opportunities through completion of prework self- and manager assessments. Finally, learning preferences appeared as level 1 reaction objectives (achieve 4.0 on a 5.0 scale on Overall Satisfaction). With this approach, the training process had built-in evaluation components, and the Career Development

Exhibit 4.7. Knowledge Test

---

(You must remember these numbers at the end of the course)

☐---☐

### Coaching and Counseling

Please, fill in this questionnaire related to the *Coaching and Counseling* course that has as its exclusive purpose to determine the level of learning reached once the course is over.

The content of this questionnaire is totally confidential. The answers of all the group members will be compiled in one document in order to protect the identity of the authors.

At the top of the document, please enter a combination of four numbers (that you must remember at the end of the course) for identification purposes.

To answer the questionnaire, you must indicate (in every item) to which extent the item really fits to team direction.

| | For the team management this behavior is | | | |
|---|---|---|---|---|
| | *Very suitable* | *Quite suitable* | *Not very suitable* | *Not suitable at all* |
| 1. Maintaining an open and personal communication with your colleagues | | | | |
| 2. Putting yourself in others' place and understanding their views | | | | |
| 3. Being polite and distant in personal relations | | | | |
| 4. Showing empathy to emotive expressions | | | | |
| 5. Considering that personal life should not be taken into account in professional life | | | | |
| 6. Respecting others' opinion | | | | |
| 7. Being inflexible with your thoughts and feelings | | | | |
| 8. Providing your colleagues with solutions in conflict situations | | | | |

*(continued)*

Exhibit 4.7. Knowledge Test (*continued*)

| | For the team management this behavior is | | | |
|---|---|---|---|---|
| | *Very suitable* | *Quite suitable* | *Not very suitable* | *Not suitable at all* |
| 9. Paying attention to others | | | | |
| 10. Understanding the real difficulties of the work of your colleagues | | | | |
| 11. Judging issues from your point of view and dismissing the others' opinions without considering feelings and emotions | | | | |
| 12. Showing indifference to the personal conflicts of your colleagues | | | | |
| 13. Ignoring whenever you can the differences and brushes between team members | | | | |
| 14. Communicating clearly and assertively | | | | |
| 15. Creating a relaxed and pleasant atmosphere suitable for dialogue | | | | |
| 16. Appearing to be perfect without having problems | | | | |
| 17. Taking care of personal relations for colleagues to be fluent and positive | | | | |
| 18. Trying to provide solutions in conflicts between personal and corporate interests | | | | |

Exhibit 4.8. Skills Test

---

**Seminar-Workshop**
**Techniques for People Management:**
**Coaching and Counseling**

----------------------------------------------------------------------

**Impulse Management or Counseling**
**Observation notes**

Name: ..........................................................................................................................

Observe the manager's behavior in regard to the verbal and the nonverbal spheres. Write down your comments for every item. At the end of the performance, grade the manager in every item and explain your scoring by writing constructive comments in the right. In the scale, 1 stands for "needs to improve substantially" and 5 stands for "excellent."

EUROSEARCH
CONSULTORES
DE
DIRECCIÓN

| CHECK LIST | COMMENTS | EXAMPLES |
|---|---|---|
| **Structure** Has the skills developer followed all the stages of the skills development model? | | |
| *In accordance with the topic | 1 2 3 4 5 | |
| *It identifies goals | 1 2 3 4 5 | |
| *It encourages discoveries | 1 2 3 4 5 | |
| *It establishes criteria | 1 2 3 4 5 | |
| *It empowers and authorizes | 1 2 3 4 5 | |
| *It recapitulates | 1 2 3 4 5 | |
| **Procedure** Has the chief used the required preparation for the procedure? | | |
| *He has paid attention carefully | 1 2 3 4 5 | |
| *He has asked questions | 1 2 3 4 5 | |
| *He has made suggestions | 1 2 3 4 5 | |
| *He has given feedback | 1 2 3 4 5 | |
| *He has used "I statements" | 1 2 3 4 5 | |

*(continued)*

Exhibit 4.8. Skills Test (*continued*)

| | | |
|---|---|---|
| **Atmosphere**<br>Has the chief created a<br>productive atmosphere?<br><br>*He has clarified purposes | 1 2 3 4 5 | |
| *He has avoided value<br>judgments<br>*He has created a pleasant,<br>genuine, respectful and<br>empathetic atmosphere<br>*Good opening and closing | 1 2 3 4 5<br><br>1 2 3 4 5<br><br><br>1 2 3 4 5 | |
| **Summary**<br>*According to you, has this<br>been a successful "Skills<br>Development" session? | 1 2 3 4 5 | |
| Has the manager followed the<br>basic counseling model?<br><br>*Exploration<br>*Finding new perspectives<br>*Action | <br><br>1 2 3 4 5<br>1 2 3 4 5<br>1 2 3 4 5 | |
| How does the manager<br>implement the basic skills<br>of counseling?<br><br>*Paying attention<br>*Listening<br>*Visual contact<br>*Nonverbal communication<br>*In the sort of questions used | <br><br><br>1 2 3 4 5<br>1 2 3 4 5<br>1 2 3 4 5<br>1 2 3 4 5<br>1 2 3 4 5 | |
| How does the manager handle<br>the two core elements in the<br>interview?<br><br>*Feelings/Emotions<br>*Empathy | <br><br><br>1 2 3 4 5<br>1 2 3 4 5 | |
| Summary<br><br>*According to you, has this<br>been a successful counseling<br>model session? | <br>1 2 3 4 5 | |

EUROSEARCH
CONSULTORES DE DIRECCIÓN

program was developed with job performance and business results in mind.

## Learning Objectives

- Define critical skills required for job effectiveness.
- Define skill gaps.
- Identify talents.
- Identify developmental needs.
- Demonstrate proficiency with development discussion guidelines.

Level 2 data were measured during the training through skill practices, role plays, and training simulations. Learning exercises focused on participants' demonstrated ability to identify the critical skills needed to execute defined performance priorities as well as participants' demonstrated ability to conduct a "development discussion" with their manager, in accordance with the development discussion guidelines provided.

Another way to evaluate Learning is to ask the participants for their feelings about what they learned. This is sometimes referred to as a "storytelling" approach to evaluation. Although this is very subjective and cannot be quantified, it can be helpful. The following approach comes from the case study of the First Union National Bank described in Chapter 3.

Because CARE was a personal development course, it was felt that both the learning and any resulting changes in behavior were of a very subjective and personal nature. To evaluate on the second and third levels (increase in learning and behavior change), the company sent a questionnaire to a random sample of the participants asking them about their learning and changes in behavior. This instrument was mailed to participants at the end of each quarter so that the longest period of time between the class and the questionnaire was about ninety days. The completed forms were returned to the Corporate Training and Development Department for processing and evaluation. Exhibit 4.9 shows the questionnaire.

Exhibit 4.9. Insti–Survey, National Computer Systems

---

*Directions:* Thank you for taking the time to complete this short survey.

Please use a No. 2 pencil.
Cleanly erase any responses you want to change.

Please use the following scale:

A = *Agree strongly*
B = *Agree somewhat*
C = *Neutral*
D = *Disagree somewhat*
E = *Disagree strongly*

*Because of my CARE Class, I*

| | | | | | |
|---|---|---|---|---|---|
| 1. Am more self-aware. | A | B | C | D | E |
| 2. Am better able to communicate with others. | A | B | C | D | E |
| 3. Am seeking more feedback on strengths and areas to improve. | A | B | C | D | E |
| 4. Feel more personally empowered. | A | B | C | D | E |
| 5. Can better respond to aggressive behavior. | A | B | C | D | E |
| 6. Can better respond to nonassertive behavior. | A | B | C | D | E |
| 7. Am more likely to assert myself now. | A | B | C | D | E |
| 8. Am better able to set goals for myself now. | A | B | C | D | E |
| 9. See how goal setting helps me make some positive changes. | A | B | C | D | E |
| 10. Feel more valued as a First Union Employee now. | A | B | C | D | E |

---

---

# Toyota Motor Sales, U.S.A., Inc.

## University of Toyota
### Judy E. Brooke, Supervisor, Measurement and Evaluation
### Gusti Lowenberg, Manager of E-Learning and M&E
### Torrance, California

The case study sent to us from our colleagues at the University of Toyota illustrates a critical point about evaluation. It is generally quite easy to use the same basic observation checklist for level 2 classroom work and then use a modified version for evaluating level 3, on-the-job observation. Their tool is displayed in Exhibit 4.10.

Exhibit 4.10. Evaluating a Performance-Improvement Program:
Service Drive Observation Checklist

| Service Advisor: | Customers in Service Drive | | | | |
|---|---|---|---|---|---|
| Team Color: | 1 | 2 | 3 | 4 | 5 |
| **DURING SERVICE WRITE-UP** | | | | | |
| Prewritten ROs for appointments | | | | | |
| Quick write-up sheet to gather info | | | | | |
| Prompt/courteous greeting (active) | | | | | |
| Introduction/customer's name | | | | | |
| Friendliness | | | | | |
| Check customer's vehicle history | | | | | |
| Listen actively to customer (eye contact) | | | | | |
| Ask open-ended questions | | | | | |
| Confirm customer's concern | | | | | |
| Educate/explain next steps | | | | | |
| Take notes while talking to customer | | | | | |
| Vehicle mileage captured | | | | | |
| Obtain/verify customer's phone number | | | | | |
| Estimate given/signature obtained | | | | | |
| Conduct vehicle walkaround | | | | | |
| Communicate walkaround to customer | | | | | |
| Use service menu | | | | | |
| Establish appropriate promise time | | | | | |
| Overcome any customer concerns about price, product, and convenience | | | | | |
| Install courtesy items on customer's vehicle | | | | | |
| **CUSTOMER CALL DURING SERVICE** | | | | | |
| All information gathered before making call | | | | | |
| If left voice mail message - concise & accurate | | | | | |
| Update/call customer to give vehicle status | | | | | |
| Reconfirm pickup/promise time | | | | | |
| Review repairs and costs with customer | | | | | |

*(continued)*

Exhibit 4.10. Evaluating a Performance-Improvement Program: Service Drive Observation Checklist *(continued)*

| Service Advisor: | Customers in Service Drive | | | | |
|---|---|---|---|---|---|
| Team Color: | 1 | 2 | 3 | 4 | 5 |
| **ACTIVE DELIVERY** | | | | | |
| Actively greet customer on return | | | | | |
| Review RO with customer | | | | | |
| Walk customer to cashier | | | | | |
| Contact customers via phone to ensure satisfaction | | | | | |

We have one final word about evaluating level 2. Do not rely on knowledge tests and/or checks to measure increase in skill-based courses. After all, we don't know about you, but we don't want our airline pilots to have simply passed a number of knowledge tests. Performance tests are necessary!

## Get a 100 Percent Response if Possible

This is the third guideline mentioned at the beginning of the chapter.

In instructor-led classes, it is usually possible to get everyone to participate. The posttest is usually administered at the end of the program before they leave.

In e-learning, it is usually not possible to get a 100 percent response unless the participants are required to pass a test, in which case the instructor needs to know the response of each person.

In programs where this is not required, the best that trainers can do is to encourage a response from each participant. This can be done by asking each participant to complete the test immediately after the program ends so that the program can be evaluated and future programs can be improved. Telling them that a 100 percent response is needed to make the evaluation valid may help to accomplish it. If the response is less than 100 percent, some kind of statistical analysis will be needed to make the evaluation valid. If the response is less than 100 percent and no statistical analysis can be made, the larger the response, the more meaningful it becomes.

## Use Evaluation Results to Take Appropriate Action

This is the final guideline described at the beginning of the chapter.

The reason for evaluating Learning is to measure to what extent the program has been effective in regard to one or more of the following objectives:

- Knowledge is learned.
- Skills are learned and/or increased.
- Attitudes are changed.

The results of the Learning evaluations, whether by tests or by observing performance in the classroom, will tell trainers how effective they have been. An analysis will show where they have and have not been effective and what changes need to be made in future programs. The answer may be one or more of the following: use different instructors, use audiovisual aids more effectively, improve the interaction with the participants, spend more time on certain topics, and improve the presentations by the present trainers.

## Summary

Surveys have been made, and the results indicate that less than half of organizations measure Learning at all for various reasons. These include lack of resources, lack of knowledge of how to do it, and/or a decision that it is not important. Sometimes they skip it and go directly to Behavior, Results, or ROI. *Don't do it!*

To get desired behavior and results, the participants need certain knowledge, skills, and attitudes. Hopefully these have been determined by analyzing the behaviors that are needed to accomplish the desired results. And it is necessary to measure learning to see if these learnings have been accomplished.

The guidelines for evaluating Learning have been stated, and a number of examples have been provided for you to consider. Choose or adapt any that you think will be useful in your organization.

A number of trainers have asked me if it is better to use the same test as a pretest and posttest or to have a Form A and B. My answer is to use the same test. It would be almost impossible to develop a Form A and B that would accurately measure the increase in knowledge or attitudes.

Two final thoughts. First, while you are checking with Human Resources to identify a statistician, check to see if they know of an expert in designing tests. You may be surprised to find someone in another department who can help.

Second, it is obvious that we have just scratched the surface regarding tests. Many books and pamphlets such as Infoline are available from the American Society for Training and Development. To find out what is available, see the contact information in The Authors section.

# Chapter 5

# Implementing Level 3: Behavior

Jim has focused a lot of his recent attention on level 3 because it is the most neglected. He refers to it as the "missing link" because of his contention that it is typically lost between levels 2 and 4. While the trend is improving, learning and training professionals still believe that their jobs are done when the training programs are over, or the computer is turned off following an e-learning session. That only takes them through level 2. Business leaders, on the other hand, most often state that their jobs are to focus on results, and that if there are problems with application of training on the job (level 3), it is a "training issue." Thus, the missing link and serious gap in actually leveraging training contribute to bottom-line results.

A popular belief is that level 4 is the most difficult level. That is sort of true and sort of false. It is false in the sense that there are lots of level 4 data available to training professionals, particularly in the form of business and human resource metrics—much more so than level 3 data. Data on sales, cost savings, turnaround times, customer and employee retention, and promotions are readily available, and most often business and HR leaders are more than willing to share it with learning professionals. However, all of these available metrics are rarely legitimately linked to training (see Chapter 6). Overall in regard to level 3, most of the organizations we are familiar with conduct little if any level 3 evaluation, stating, "It is too difficult," "It is too expensive," or "We don't have the resources to do it." We believe that level 3 does not have to be difficult.

There are three reasons to take a serious look at evaluating level 3.

First, the acquisition of knowledge and skills translates to little actual business value unless they are transferred to new on-the-job behaviors. After all, how are results supposed to be realized but through targeted action? Failure to conduct level 3 evaluation will decrease the likelihood that this transfer takes place. We find that effective level 3 evaluation acts as a reinforcer of new behaviors.

Case in point: Recent attempts by terrorists to blow up U.S.-bound airplanes with mixtures of liquids has caused the Transportation Safety Authority (TSA) to implement immediate procedures to check carry-on baggage and forbid seating-area transport of all liquids and gels over 3 ounces. Immediate and urgent training was administered to thousands of TSA employees within a few days. Shortly after this new screening process went into effect, I (Jim) was in the airport and my carry-on bag was checked. A TSC worker unzipped my bag, searched it, zipped it back up, and wished me a nice trip. His supervisor had been observing him and before I could take a step courteously said, "Hold it, sir!" She reopened my bag and pulled out a can of shaving cream, and said, "I am sorry. This is too big and you will either have to check it or leave it with us." She then explained to the first TSA worker why she had flagged it.

Let us ask you this—do you think it would have been a good idea for TSA to wait thirty days to see if the learnings had transferred to new behavior? Certainly not! In this case, level 3 evaluation—in this instance, on-the-job observation using a checklist—needed to be implemented immediately to *ensure* that the transfer took place. I (Jim, again) was in an airport the other day and was talking with a group of TSA employees about their jobs. I asked them about new rules and procedures and they said, "After we are trained, our supervisors don't wait five minutes before they are evaluating us to make sure we are performing our new duties correctly." This is a very common business situation where immediate level 3 evaluation can act as a terrific reinforcer of new behaviors that would never take root without it. This notion is supported by the common suggestion after training to "make sure you apply what you learned as soon as you get the opportunity." We are merely saying that early evaluation at level 3 can help ensure that occurs.

Second, level 3 is the only way to tell if lack of success at level 4 is caused by ineffective training or lack of sufficient follow-up. It is our belief that poor training results more often come from lack of follow-up than from poor training programs or delivery. That is why we consistently recommend to evaluators that when conducting level 3 evaluation with program participants, some effort is made to query whether a failure to effectively apply what was learned was due to irrelevant or inappropriate training, or to an unsupportive working atmosphere. All too often, the snag is with the supervisors and culture failing to support and reinforce learnings, yet the complaint is often "ineffective training."

Third, it is extremely difficult to create a compelling *chain of evidence* leading from training to results without it (see Chapter 7 for details on our chain of evidence). The appropriate blend of data and information from each of the first three levels is necessary to be able to tell the story of value through evaluation. Specifically, we believe the best way to demonstrate the value of learning to stakeholders is to present a "show-and-tell" that goes something like this:

> Here are data that show that our learners were engaged in the training and found it relevant (level 1), which led to an increase in knowledge and skills (level 2), which with the support and involvement from your fine leaders helped lead to significant changes in behavior (level 3), which ultimately contributed to the results you were looking for (level 4).

Without the targeted application of mission-critical behaviors, that complete story could not be told, and evaluating at level 3 is just the ticket to complete the chain to level 4.

Many learning professionals are also limited by what they know to be actual level 3 methods. We believe that there are no less than four great ways to evaluate at level 3. They are the following:

1. *Surveys and questionnaires*: Likert scale and open-ended questions that can be asked of anyone who observes the behavior of employees on the job.
2. *Observation and checklists*: consist of someone actually observing the employee on the job, and typically refer to a table of the behaviors that are being assessed.
3. *Work review*: reviewing actual work that has been completed by the trainees on the job without actually observing them doing it.

4. *Interviews and focus groups*: consist of structured questions that can be administered to either individuals (interview) or groups (focus groups) to query to what degree new behaviors are being applied on the job. Follow-up questions to action plans are an excellent way to administer this.

Evaluating level 3 means measuring changes in behavior caused by the training program. Let us assume you have measured level 2, either during or after a program, and are now ready to measure level 3. You have determined that the participants have acquired new knowledge related to their jobs, learned new skills related to their jobs, and/or changed their attitudes that could have a positive effect on their job performance. Now it is time to see whether these changes have transferred to the job.

In the previous chapter, we described a change in the attitudes of the learners regarding the way to make decisions on the job. The learners (executives at ServiceMaster in Downers Grove, Illinois) stated that they were going to make decisions using more input from subordinates than they had previously done. Will they follow through in their behavior, or will they keep doing what they had been doing before they attended the training program? The questions become "What happens when trainees leave the classroom and return to their jobs? How much transfer of knowledge, skills, and attitudes occur?" That is what level 3 attempts to evaluate. In other words, what change in job behavior occurred because people attended a training program?

It is obvious that this question is more complicated and difficult to answer than evaluating at the first two levels. First, trainees cannot change their behavior until they have an opportunity to do so. For example, if you, the reader of this book, decide to use some of the principles and techniques that we have described, you must wait until you have a training program to evaluate. Likewise, if the training program is designed to teach a person how to conduct an effective performance appraisal interview, the trainee cannot apply the learning until an interview is held.

Second, it is impossible to predict when a change in behavior will occur. Even if a trainee has an opportunity to apply the learning, he or she may not do it immediately. In fact, change in behavior may occur at any time after the first opportunity, or it may never occur. That is why, of course, we mentioned the importance of early level 3 evaluation for mission-critical behaviors.

Third, the trainee may apply the learning to the job and come to one of the following conclusions:

"I like what happened, and I plan to continue to use the new behavior."

"I don't like what happened, and I will go back to my old behavior."

"I like what happened, but my supervisor and/or time restraints prevent me from continuing it."

We all hope that the rewards for changing behavior will cause the trainee to come to the first of these conclusions. It is important, therefore, to provide help, encouragement, and reinforcement when the trainee returns to the job from the training class. One type of reinforcement is "intrinsic." This term refers to the inward feelings of satisfaction, pride, achievement, and happiness that can occur when the new behavior is used. Intrinsic reinforcement, leading to internal motivation, is generally longer lasting than extrinsic (external) reinforcement. However, intrinsic reinforcement by itself rarely is enough to get a group of employees behaving in a new way.

Thus, extrinsic reinforcement is also important. These are the reinforcers that come from the outside. They include praise, increased freedom and empowerment, merit pay increases, and other forms of recognition that are administered as the result of the change in behavior. Typically, a balance of internal and external reinforcers is needed to facilitate group behavior change and subsequent positive results. In regard to reaction and learning, the evaluation typically takes place either during or immediately after training. When you evaluate change in behavior, there are more variables and factors to consider when deciding how and when to administer level 3 methods. This potentially makes it more time-consuming and difficult to do than levels 1 and 2. Here are some guidelines to follow when evaluating at level 3.

## Guidelines for Evaluating Behavior

1. Use a control group if practical.
2. Allow time for the on-the-job behavior to be performed.
3. Evaluate both before and after the program if practical.
4. Consider a variety of methods. If you use surveys and/or interviews, consider one or more of the following who have an opportunity to observe the trainee's behavior:
   - trainees themselves
   - immediate supervisor
   - direct reports
   - peers
   - customers
5. Get a 100 percent response or a sampling.
6. Repeat the evaluation at appropriate times.
7. Consider cost versus benefits.

The remainder of this chapter suggests ways of implementing these guidelines.

## Use a Control Group if Practical

Chapter 4 described the use of control groups in detail. A comparison of the change in behavior of a control group with the change experienced by the experimental group can add evidence that the change in behavior occurred because of the training program and not for other reasons. It will be difficult at best or impossible at worst to find or create groups that are statistically equivalent. Whether to go forward with a control group depends on how credible the data need to be. If you are looking for general comparisons between two similar groups, and there is not a statistician in high power that will shred any data below a statistically significant level of .95, then you might want to go for it. An example that Jim brings to mind was a bank he worked with on a new sales methodology. Fifteen customer branches were trained on the method of customer profiling, and twenty were not. The bank's business leaders were satisfied with data that came from the two groups, knowing that the findings were estimates. Decisions were made to move forward with the training with all of the branches, as the data strongly suggested that the new method was better than what customer service reps had been doing. It is important to note that a variety of level 3 and level 4 metrics were used to evaluate the effectiveness of the sales training, not just the comparison of the two groups.

## Allow Time for Behavior Change to Take Place

As already indicated, no evaluation should be attempted until trainees have had an opportunity to use the new behavior on the job. We stated earlier that sometimes there is an immediate opportunity for applying it on the job. The new TSA rules for carrying liquids on airplanes, discussed above, is one. Others would include diversity training, customer service skills, and management by walking around (MBWA), as encouraged by United Airlines and Hewlett-Packard. However, if the purpose of the training is to teach a foreman how to handle a grievance, no change in behavior is possible until a grievance has been filed. Again, it is important to understand that while the *opportunity* to evaluate at level 3 often presents itself immediately, the *decision* to evaluate at level 3 is that sometimes it is important to begin it immediately (i.e., for mission-critical behaviors), and sometimes it is best to wait until new behaviors have had a chance to take root. Two or three months after training are a good rule of thumb. For others, six months is more realistic.

## Evaluate Both Before and After the Program if Practical

Measuring behavior before and after a program is the best way to determine how much the behavior had changed as a result of the program. Sometimes evaluation before and after a program is practical, and sometimes it is not even possible. For example, supervisors who attend the Management Institute of the University of Wisconsin training programs sometimes do not enroll until a day or two before the program starts. It would not be possible for the instructors or designated research students to measure their behavior before the program. In an in-house program, it would be possible, but it might not be practical because of time and budget constraints.

For example, it is important when planning a supervisory training program to determine the kind of behavior that supervisors should have in order to be most effective. Before the training program, you measure the behavior of the supervisors. After the program, at a time to be determined as just outlined, you measure the behavior of the supervisors again to see whether any change has taken place in relation to the knowledge, skills, and/or attitudes that the training program taught. By comparing the behaviors observed before and after the program, you can determine any change that has taken place, and attribute at least some of it to the training.

An alternative approach can also be effective. Under this approach, you measure behavior after the program only. Those whom you interview or survey are asked to identify any behavior that was different than it had been before the program. This was the approach that we used at the Management Institute to evaluate the three-day supervisory training program called Developing Supervisory Skills. Chapter 14 in *Evaluating Training Programs*, third edition, describes this evaluation.

## Survey and/or Interview Persons Who Know and Observe the Behavior

As this guideline suggests, level 3 data and information are only worthwhile if they come from individuals who personally observe the behavior or the work that is performed by the trainees. The term "360 degree feedback" is familiar to most learning professionals and is the best example of this guideline in action. In order to get a variety of data, evaluators should consider assessing more than one of the following: trainees, their immediate supervisor, their direct reports, their peers, and their customers (internal or external).

Four questions need to be considered when deciding whom to evaluate:

1.  Who is best qualified to provide accurate data and/or information?

If we try to determine who is best qualified, the answer is probably the direct reports who see the behavior of the trainee on a regular basis. In some cases, others who are neither boss nor direct reports have regular contact with the trainee. And, of course, the trainee has some awareness of his or her own behavior. The immediate supervisor may or may not be the best person to evaluate the trainee depending on the amount of time he or she actually spends with the trainee.

2. Who is the most reliable?

The trainee may be reluctant to admit that his or her behavior has not changed. Direct reports can be biased in favor of or against the trainee and therefore give a distorted picture. In fact, anyone can give a distorted picture, depending on his or her attitude toward the trainee or the program. This is why more than one source should be used.

3. Who is the most available?

The answer depends on the particular situation. Jim was recently talking with training professionals from a very successful U.S.-based airline, and the question came up, "How should we conduct our level 3s of behaviors of flight attendants and ticketing agents?" After commending them on their interest and effort directed toward level 3 (Jim's favorite level, by the way), they went down the list of possibilities. Other flight attendants would not work so well, as there were political and union reasons against it; pilots were not such a hot idea since they would be busy flying the plane; supervisors were ruled out, as they could not spend enough time in the air to supply good data; and Federal Aviation Administration (FAA) personnel do conduct audits, but have their own criteria that they are observing. Jim stated, "Well, it seems to me that you have a huge potential population standing by and *available* that could do the job. How about us—the passengers?" The airline professionals responded that a third party already did collect some level 3 data, but "only one question really applies to the behavior of either the ticketing agents or the flight attendants." After some further discussion, they decided to see if a form could be developed and sent to customers that would indeed provide useful level 3 information. If interviews are to be conducted, then availability is critical. If a survey questionnaire is used, it is not important. In this case, the answer depends on who is willing to spend the time needed to complete the survey.

4. How many sources of level 3 data and information should be used?

It is considered a best practice in the human resource industry to obtain data from more than one source for employee performance appraisals. The rationale is that multiple data points provide a more complete and accurate picture of the employee's actual performance than does any one source. The same is true for level 3 evaluation. We generally frown on only considering, for instance, self-assessments of the trainees. Too much bias can be encountered. And, the comparisons of different sources of level 3 data are often very enlightening as to what is really happening in terms of the transfer of learning to behavior.

Are there any reasons why one or more of the possible candidates should not be used in assessing level 3? The answer is yes. For example, asking direct reports for information on the behavior of their supervisor may not set well with the supervisor. However, if the trainee is willing to have his or her direct reports questioned, this may be the best approach of all.

A significant decision is whether to use a questionnaire, an interview, or a focus group. Both have their advantages and disadvantages. Questionnaires and surveys tend to provide more *data*, while interviews and focus groups tend to provide richer *information*. We suggest the use of a patterned questionnaire for interviews and focus groups in which all interviewees are asked the same questions. Then you can tabulate the responses and gather quantitative data on behavior change. But interviews and focus groups are very time-consuming, and only a few can be conducted if the availability of the person doing the evaluating is limited. Therefore, a small sample of those trained can be interviewed. However, the sample may not be representative of the behavior change that took place in trainees. And you cannot draw conclusions about the overall change in behavior. Exhibit 5.1 shows a patterned interview that can be used as is or adapted to your particular situation.

A survey questionnaire is usually more practical. If it is designed properly, it can provide the data that you need to evaluate change in behavior. The usual problem of getting people to take the time to complete it is always present. Adequate sample size is a frequent concern. However, you can attack this challenge by several methods. First,

Exhibit 5.1. Patterned Interview

---

The interviewer reviews the program with the interviewee and highlights the behaviors that the program encouraged. The interviewer then clarifies the purpose of the interview, which is to evaluate the effectiveness of the course so that improvements can be made in the future. Specifically, the interview will determine the extent to which the suggested behaviors have been applied on the job. If they have not been applied, the interview will seek to learn why not. The interviewer makes it clear that all information will be held confidential so that the answers given can be frank and honest.

1.  What specific behaviors were you taught and encouraged to use?

2.  When you left the program, how eager were you to change your behavior on the job?

    \_\_\_\_\_ Very eager    \_\_\_\_\_ Quite eager    \_\_\_\_\_ Not eager

    Comments:

3.  How well equipped were you to do what was suggested?

    \_\_\_\_\_ Very    \_\_\_\_\_ Quite    \_\_\_\_\_ Little    \_\_\_\_\_ None

4.  If you are <u>not doing</u> some of the things that you were encouraged and taught to do, why not?

|  | How Significant? | | |
|---|---|---|---|
|  | *Very* | *To some extent* | *Not* |
| a.  It wasn't practical for my situation. |  |  |  |
| b.  My boss discourages me from changing. |  |  |  |
| c.  I haven't found the time. |  |  |  |
| d.  I tried it, and it didn't work. |  |  |  |
| e.  Other reasons. |  |  |  |

5.  To what extent do you plan to do things differently in the future?

    \_\_\_\_\_ Large extent    \_\_\_\_\_ Some extent    \_\_\_\_\_ No extent

6.  What suggestions do you have for making the program more helpful?

---

be sure to pre-position the trainees and others who will be evaluating them by sharing during the program what will be done to gather level 3 data, and why. The best general approach is to say something like the following:

> This training and the new skills that you will learn are critical to our success going forward. Applying these skills to on-the-job behaviors will not only help you develop yourselves professionally, but also allow us to serve our customers better. Therefore, we are going to provide several opportunities for you to be observed and report on your progress following the conclusion of the program so that we can help you apply your learnings if there are any snags. We do this because we care!!

If the belief is strong that level 3 is being done, not to watch over people and catch them as they make errors, but to help them to improve their performance, sample size and honesty will increase.

Second, we can increase sample size by offering some type of reinforcement to the people whom you ask to complete the surveys or conduct observations. Perhaps there can be some reward, either intrinsic or extrinsic, for doing it. Or a person can be motivated to do it as a favor to the person doing the research. Producing information for top management as the reason for doing it may convince some. If the instructor, the person doing the evaluation, or both have built a rapport with those who are asked to complete the survey, they usually will cooperate. Exhibit 5.2 shows a survey questionnaire that you can use as is or adapt to your organization.

## Get 100 Percent Response or a Sampling

The dictum that something beats nothing can apply when you evaluate change in behavior. The person doing the evaluation can pick out a few "typical" trainees at random and interview, survey, or observe them. Or you can interview or survey the persons most likely not to change. The conclusion might be that, if Joe and Charlie have changed their behavior, then everyone has. This conclusion may or may not be true, but the approach can be practical. Obviously, the best approach is to measure the behavior change in all trainees. In most cases, this is not

Exhibit 5.2. Survey Questionnaire

---

*Instructions:* The purpose of this questionnaire is to determine the extent to which those who attended the recent program on leadership methods have applied the principles and techniques that they learned there to the job. The results of the survey will help us to assess the effectiveness of the program and identify ways in which it can be made more practical for those who attend. Please be frank and honest in your answers. Your name is strictly optional. The only reason we ask is that we might want to follow up on your answers to get more comments and suggestions from you.

Please circle the appropriate response after each question.

5 = Much more   4 = Some more   3 = The same   2 = Some less   1 = Much less

| *Understanding and Motivating* | Time and energy spent after the program compared to time and energy spent before the program | | | | |
|---|---|---|---|---|---|
| 1.  Getting to know my employees | 5 | 4 | 3 | 2 | 1 |
| 2.  Listening to my subordinates | 5 | 4 | 3 | 2 | 1 |
| 3.  Praising good work | 5 | 4 | 3 | 2 | 1 |
| 4.  Talking with employees about their families and other personal interests | 5 | 4 | 3 | 2 | 1 |
| 5.  Asking subordinates for their ideas | 5 | 4 | 3 | 2 | 1 |
| 6.  Managing by walking around | 5 | 4 | 3 | 2 | 1 |
| *Orienting and Training* | | | | | |
| 7.  Asking new employees about their families, past experience, etc. | 5 | 4 | 3 | 2 | 1 |
| 8.  Taking new employees on a tour of the department and other facilities | 5 | 4 | 3 | 2 | 1 |
| 9.  Introducing new employees to their coworkers | 5 | 4 | 3 | 2 | 1 |
| 10. Using the four-step method when training new and present employees | 5 | 4 | 3 | 2 | 1 |
| 11. Being patient when employees don't learn as fast as I think they should | 5 | 4 | 3 | 2 | 1 |
| 12. Tactfully correcting mistakes and making suggestions | 5 | 4 | 3 | 2 | 1 |
| 13. Using the training inventory and timetable concept | 5 | 4 | 3 | 2 | 1 |

What would have made the program more practical and helpful to you?

Name (optional) _____

practical. Each organization must determine the amount of time and money that it can spend on level 3 evaluation and proceed accordingly.

## Repeat the Evaluation at Appropriate Times

Some trainees may change their behavior as soon as they return to their job. This usually occurs because of their strong internal motivation and/or immediate coaching or evaluation. Others may wait six months or a year, or never change. And those who change immediately may revert to the old behavior after trying out the new behavior for a period of time. Therefore, it is important to repeat the evaluation at an appropriate time. We cannot stress enough that regular evaluation not only serves to provide data on an ongoing basis that can be acted on, but also acts as a continual reinforcer. Again, many trainees will simply stop performing the desired behaviors if they know that no one is noticing.

We wish we could describe an appropriate time to repeat level 3 evaluation. Each organization has to make the decision on its own, taking into account the importance and kind of behavior, the job climate, and other significant factors unique to the situation. For non-mission-critical behaviors, we would suggest waiting two or three months before conducting the first evaluation, the exact number depending on the opportunity that trainees have to use the new behavior. Perhaps another six months should elapse before the evaluation is repeated. And, depending on circumstances and the time available, a third evaluation could be made three to six months later. In some cases, for example where changes in skills have been taught, the first evaluation should be made much sooner than three months, perhaps within a week. We know of many companies who routinely reevaluate level 3 at 30–60–90 days, yet may not have a good rationale for doing so.

## Consider Costs versus Benefits

Just as with other investments, you should compare the cost of evaluating change in behavior with the benefits that could result from the evaluation. In many organizations, much of the cost of evaluation at level 3 is in the staff time that it takes to do it. And time is money. Other costs of evaluation can include the hiring of an outside expert to guide or even conduct the evaluation. For example, I (Don) have been hired by Kemper Insurance, Ford, GE, Blockbuster, and Northern States Power to present and discuss the four levels of evaluation with their training staff. At Kemper, I was asked to offer specific suggestions and return three months later to comment on the evaluations that they had done. In these instances, I was called in not to evaluate a specific program, but to provide guidelines and specific suggestions on how programs could be evaluated at all four levels. Other consultants can be called in to evaluate the changes in behavior that result from a specific program. You should consider such costs as these when you decide whether to evaluate changes in behavior.

The other factor to consider is the benefits that can be derived from evaluation, including changes in behavior and final results. The greater the potential benefits, the more time and money can be spent on the evaluation, not only of behavior change but in level 4 also. Specific factors that, in our opinion, beg for robust level 3 evaluation include the following:

1. The new behaviors are critical to the execution of organizational strategy.
2. The program is a pilot, and it is important to know if the behaviors can be realistically applied to the job.
3. The program is one of high visibility and/or impact, and therefore it will be important to have a complete chain of evidence to demonstrate value.
4. The behaviors are very different from what participants are used to doing, and thus require a lot of reinforcement.
5. The program will be repeated on a frequent basis, and it is important to ensure that the behaviors are really leading to desired outcomes (level 4).
6. Any type of leadership or coaching behaviors that will leverage the success of all other training.

It is important to understand that change in behavior is not an end in itself. Rather, it is a means to an end: the final results that can be achieved if change in behavior occurs. If no change in behavior occurs, then no improved results can occur as a result of the training program. At the same time, even if change in behavior does occur, positive results may not be achieved.

A good example is the principle and technique of Managing by Walking Around (MBWA). Some organizations, including United Airlines and Hewlett-Packard, found that higher morale and increased productivity can result from MBWA. These organizations therefore encouraged managers at all levels to walk among the lowest-level employees to show that they care. Picture a manager—Charlie—who has never shown concern for people. He attends a seminar at which he is told to change his behavior by walking around among his direct reports to show that he cares. So Charlie—for the first time—changes his behavior. He asks one employee about the kids. He comments to another employee regarding a vacation trip that the employee's family is planning. And he asks another employee about Sam, the pet dog. (The manager has learned about these things before talking to the three employees.) What are the chances that the three employees are now going to be motivated to increase their productivity because the manager really cares? Or will they look with suspicion on the new behavior and wonder what the boss is up to? The manager's change in behavior could even have negative results.

This possibility underlines the fact that some behavior encouraged in the classroom is not appropriate for all participants. Encouraging supervisors to empower employees is a behavior that would not be appropriate in departments that had a lot of new employees, employees with negative attitudes, or employees with limited knowledge.

Let us look at specific samples of level 3 evaluation tools.

## Surveys

The first example is from First Union National Bank out of Charlotte, North Carolina. This simple survey (simple is oftentimes best) addresses some of the specific skills covered in their CARE program, which was designed to assist nonexempt employees with personal and professional development issues. See Exhibit 4.8.

The Gap Inc. provides us with two complementary surveys. Two to three months after the program Leadership Training for Supervisors, trainers surveyed both the store managers who attended and their immediate subordinates. Exhibit 5.3 illustrates the form used for the store managers, and 5.4 is the one for their direct reports.

In the U.S. Geological Survey Leadership Development case study, they described their approach to measuring behavior as follows:

Exhibit 5.3. LTS Post–Program Survey: Store Manager Version

---

Store Manager _____ Division _____

This survey is designed to describe your experiences with your employees since completing the LTS program. Please answer the questions by identifying the number that corresponds to your response.

|  | Much better | Somewhat better | No change | Somewhat worse | Much worse | Don't know |
|---|---|---|---|---|---|---|

Since attending the LTS program,

| | | | | | | |
|---|---|---|---|---|---|---|
| 1. How would you describe your ability to look at a situation and assess the development level of your employees? (e.g., skills, knowledge, past experience, interest, confidence level, etc.) | 6 | 5 | 4 | 3 | 2 | 1 |

Comments:

| | | | | | | |
|---|---|---|---|---|---|---|
| 2. How effective are you with choosing the most appropriate leadership style to use to develop your employees' skills and motivation? | 6 | 5 | 4 | 3 | 2 | 1 |

Comments:

| | | | | | | |
|---|---|---|---|---|---|---|
| 3. How would you describe your ability to use a variety of the four leadership styles comfortably? | 6 | 5 | 4 | 3 | 2 | 1 |

Comments:

| | | | | | | |
|---|---|---|---|---|---|---|
| 4. How is your ability to provide direction? (e.g., setting clear goals, training, setting priorities, defining standards, etc.) | 6 | 5 | 4 | 3 | 2 | 1 |

Comments:

| | | | | | | |
|---|---|---|---|---|---|---|
| 5. How is your ability to provide support? (e.g., praising, trusting employees, explaining why, listening, allowing mistakes, encouraging, etc.) | 6 | 5 | 4 | 3 | 2 | 1 |

Comments:

| | | | | | | |
|---|---|---|---|---|---|---|
| 6. How is your ability to reach agreement with your employees about the leadership style they need from you in order to complete a task or goal? | 6 | 5 | 4 | 3 | 2 | 1 |

Comments:

*(continued)*

Exhibit 5.3. LTS Post-Program Survey: Store Manager Version (*continued*)

| | Much better | Somewhat better | No change | Somewhat worse | Much worse | Don't know |
|---|---|---|---|---|---|---|
| 7. To what extent have your listening skills changed? (e.g., encouraging dialogue, concentrating, clarifying, and confirming) | 6 | 5 | 4 | 3 | 2 | 1 |
| Comments: | | | | | | |
| 8. How would you describe your ability to communicate information in a clear and specific manner? | 6 | 5 | 4 | 3 | 2 | 1 |
| Comments: | | | | | | |
| 9. How are your skills with creating clear goals with your employees? | 6 | 5 | 4 | 3 | 2 | 1 |
| Comments: | | | | | | |
| 10. How would you describe your ability to provide timely, significant, and specific *positive* feedback? | 6 | 5 | 4 | 3 | 2 | 1 |
| Comments: | | | | | | |
| 11. How would your describe your ability to provide timely, significant, and specific *constructive* feedback? | 6 | 5 | 4 | 3 | 2 | 1 |
| Comments: | | | | | | |
| 12. To what extent have you changed with providing recognition for employee accomplishments? | 6 | 5 | 4 | 3 | 2 | 1 |
| Comments: | | | | | | |

Our questionnaires seek a wide variety of behavioral self-reports from participants, and these are complemented by identical questions asked of evaluators, who have been asked to comment on the participants. The survey incorporates a large group of behavioral measures, and these are repeated in multiple surveys to provide pre-post and treatment-control comparisons.

Exhibit 5.4. LTS Post-Program Survey: Associate/Assistant Manager Version

---

Associate/Assistant Manager_____ Division _____

This survey is designed to describe your experiences with your store manager since their completing the LTS program. Please answer the questions by identifying the number that corresponds to your response.

| | Much better | Somewhat better | No change | Somewhat worse | Much worse | Don't know |
|---|---|---|---|---|---|---|

Since your store manager attended
the LTS program,

1. How would you describe their ability     6     5     4     3     2     1
   to look at a situation and assess your skills,
   knowledge, past experience, interest,
   confidence level, etc.?

   Comments:

2. How effective have they been with     6     5     4     3     2     1
   helping you develop your skills
   and motivating you?

   Comments:

3. How would you describe their ability     6     5     4     3     2     1
   to use a "different strokes for different
   folks" approach when helping you
   accomplish a task or goal?

   Comments:

4. How would you describe their ability     6     5     4     3     2     1
   to provide you direction when needed?
   (e.g., setting clear goals, training, setting
   priorities, defining standards, etc.)

   Comments:

5. How would you describe their ability     6     5     4     3     2     1
   to provide you support when needed?
   (e.g., praising, trusting, explaining
   why, listening, allowing mistakes,
   encouraging, etc.)

   Comments:

6. How is their ability to reach agreement     6     5     4     3     2     1
   with you about what you need in order
   to complete a task or goal?

   Comments:

*(continued)*

Exhibit 5.4. LTS Post-Program Survey: Associate/Assistant
Manager Version (*continued*)

| | Much better | Somewhat better | No change | Somewhat worse | Much worse | Don't know |
|---|---|---|---|---|---|---|
| 7. To what extent do they listen to what you say? | 6 | 5 | 4 | 3 | 2 | 1 |
| Comments: | | | | | | |
| 8. How would you describe their ability to communicate information that is clear and specific? | 6 | 5 | 4 | 3 | 2 | 1 |
| Comments: | | | | | | |
| 9. How have their skills changed with creating clear goals with you? | 6 | 5 | 4 | 3 | 2 | 1 |
| Comments: | | | | | | |
| 10. How would you describe their ability to provide timely, significant, and specific *positive* feedback? | 6 | 5 | 4 | 3 | 2 | 1 |
| Comments: | | | | | | |
| 11. How would you describe their ability to provide timely, significant, and specific *constructive* feedback? | 6 | 5 | 4 | 3 | 2 | 1 |
| Comments: | | | | | | |
| 12. To what extent have they changed with recognizing your accomplishments? | 6 | 5 | 4 | 3 | 2 | 1 |
| Comments: | | | | | | |

*When working with other people, how likely are you to:*                    Not very–Very

| | | | | | |
|---|---|---|---|---|---|
| a. Retreat from a (potentially conflictual) situation? | 1 | 2 | 3 | 4 | 5 |
| b. Hold team members accountable? | 1 | 2 | 3 | 4 | 5 |
| c. Communicate effectively with colleagues? | 1 | 2 | 3 | 4 | 5 |

d. Volunteer for a leadership role?                1  2  3  4  5
e. Maintain focus/intensity when you're
   confronted with adversity?                      1  2  3  4  5

*How effectively do you think you:*              Not very–Very

a. Coach and mentor?                               1  2  3  4  5
b. Listen to ideas and concerns?                   1  2  3  4  5
c. Think and plan strategically?                   1  2  3  4  5
d. Keep everyone focused on the purpose
   of the team?                                    1  2  3  4  5

*In your estimation, how much do you:*             Little–Lots

a. Open yourself up for feedback?                  1  2  3  4  5
b. Commit to improving areas of weakness?          1  2  3  4  5
c. Work to maintain the goals and objectives
   of the USGS?                                    1  2  3  4  5
d. Actively support others?                        1  2  3  4  5

## Questionnaires

The Regence Group provides us with an excellent questionnaire that is used as a level 3 tool for one of their Technology Skills Training programs. This tool can be used as an interview form or a written questionnaire. (See Exhibit 5.5.)

The University of Toyota developed a questionnaire to evaluate on-the-job behavior for a performance improvement program that dealt with labor sales and efficiencies. The questionnaire, to be filled out by a manager, can be used as a before-and-after instrument. (See Exhibit 5.6.)

## Observation Checklists

The checklist in Exhibit 4.10 was also supplied to us by the University of Toyota for their labor performance improvement case study. It is to be filled out through observation by the manager of the training participant.

Exhibit 5.5. Part B Levels 1, 2, and 3 Online Assessment

---

INSTRUCTIONS: When you have completed this evaluation, click Submit.

Course name and objectives

Your name:

Questions

Choices: a. To a very great extent  b. To a great extent  c. To a moderate extent
d. To a small extent  e. Not at all/never/rarely applicable  f. Not applicable

1.  To what extent did you use the knowledge and/or skills prior to attending this course?
2.  To what extent have you had the opportunity to use the knowledge and/or skills presented in this course?
3.  To what extent have you actually used the knowledge and/or skills presented in this course, after completing the course?
4.  To what extent has your confidence in using the knowledge and/or skills increased as a result of this course?
5.  To what extent did you receive the assistance necessary in preparing you for this course?
6.  To what extent has the content of this course accurately reflected what happens on the job?
7.  To what extent have you had access to the necessary resources (e.g., equipment and information) to apply the knowledge and/or skills on your job?
8.  To what extent have you received help, through coaching and/or feedback, with applying the knowledge and/or skills on the job?
9.  As a result of this course, my performance on the course objectives has changed by (%).
10.  As a result of this course, my overall job performance has changed by (%).

---

PacifiCorp also provides us with a second on-the-job observation checklist (see Exhibit 4.4). Their program, on procedures for managing a power outage, is set up perfectly for this tool.

## Focus Groups

We recommend focus groups when it is important to get a lot of information about how well the learnings from a program are being applied on the job. These can be conducted with equal effectiveness

Exhibit 5.6. Evaluating a Performance-Improvement Program: Service Manager
Pretraining Interview Worksheet

---

Name of Service Manager:

What factors in your dealership environment seem to make it easy or difficult to put
into practice what you learn at a class?

_____

_____

_____

_____

_____

_____

Do you think management supports your personal training?

_____

_____

_____

_____

Do you have a process in place in the service department for the ASMs activities
during the course of a day? If so, what is the process and how was it communicated
to them?

_____

_____

_____

_____

_____

Do your ASMs make their own service appointments?

_____

_____

_____

What percent of your business do you think is appointments? _____

Are appointments staggered throughout the day? _____

Do the ASMs conduct a vehicle walkaround when writing up service? _____

Do the ASMs use service menus? _____

_____

_____

Are the ASMs instructed to contact customers during the day to provide a status of
the vehicle? _____

_____

_____

Do the ASMs call the customer to explain the repairs or wait until they pick up
their car? _____

_____

_____

_____

with participants, managers, or direct reports. The Canada Revenue Agency came up with a list of issues (below) that can easily be converted into focus group questions. We suggest you use the categories to develop your questions.

### Appreciative Inquiry

- Discovering new ways of doing things
- Reflecting more

### Managing Priorities

- Learning how to say no
- Beating the terror of e-mails
- Learning to distinguish between urgent and important
- Being better organized
- Being more available for team members

### Managing Meetings

- Encouraging participation
- Rotating meeting functions
- Doing joint minutes with a related team
- Being better organized

### Performance Management

- Being more effective at career management
- Helping to get buy-in to performance management process

### Armchair Session

- Being yourself
- Treating others the way you want to be treated

### Coaching

- Investigating the commitment behind the complaint

## Summary

Evaluating level 3, Behavior, is the most difficult and time-consuming of the four levels. And make no mistake about it—it is the missing link between training and results. We have described some guidelines and techniques for doing it. It can be done through surveys, questionnaires, interviews, observed behaviors, observation of work, and focus groups. The approach you use will depend on your resources and your desire to do it.

Whatever method you use, be sure to get honest answers. For example, if you interview the trainees, they may be reluctant to say they have not implemented any of the learning because it will make them look bad. It is important to stress that you are measuring the effectiveness of the program and trying to determine to what extent it has been practical. Stress that their answers may help to improve future programs. Also, tell them that their answers will remain anonymous so they feel no pressure to say they have made changes when they have not.

Remember this: Do not try to measure results until you first measure changes in behavior. If you skip this level, there is no way of knowing whether the final results came from the training program or from other sources. Finally, if you get good at this, you will find the truth in the statement, "If you do a good job with levels 1, 2, and 3, level 4 generally takes care of itself."

# Chapter 6

## Implementing Level 4: Results

We want to be very clear about level 4. The Kirkpatrick view of results differs from many of the other views of demonstrating the results of training to the bottom line. We believe in the business partnership model of linking training to results—that is, the partnership between learning professionals and business leaders and their needs. We are *not* isolationists. We put relatively little emphasis on using estimates and assumptions (and perhaps some smoke and mirrors) to try to isolate the effects of training. First of all, we believe isolation methods and formulas reinforce the "us versus them" mentality that keeps business leaders from seeing the true usefulness and contribution learning plays in the execution of their strategies. Second, we find that most business executives and line-of-business leaders are more convinced by multiple sources of evidence that learning has indeed made a significant contribution to their results. Finally, we are not sure that it is mathematically sound to take estimates and assumptions and convert them into hard numbers—such as cost-benefit ratios. Anyway, if you are interested in calculating some such ratio, feel free to review the work of some of our colleagues, as you will not find it in the succeeding pages of this chapter.

Many people believe that level 4 is the most important and most difficult. We believe in the first statement but not the second. It is the most important to our stakeholders (our business partners). Therefore, it needs to be the most important to us (as learning professionals). It is *not* all that hard, however. The data and information that represent level 4 are not difficult to come by. The challenge is to link the level

4 Results with training. Hang in there, and we will explain how to do so in detail.

Trainers are typically faced with questions like these:

- How much did quality improve because of the training program on new generation leadership that we have presented to all supervisors and managers?
- How much did productivity increase because we conducted a program on personal effectiveness in the workforce for all employees?
- What has been the result of all our programs on new customer service methods on customer retention?
- How much have costs been reduced because we implemented a new e-learning program on setting priorities and budgeting?
- What tangible benefits have we received for all the money we have spent on programs on career development?
- How much have sales increased as the result of teaching our salespeople techniques of relationship selling?
- What have been the results of our new course on critical thinking in the battlefield?

These and similar questions illustrate an increasing pressure from executives to show the value of training. If they are asking these questions, we want you to be prepared to be able to answer them. If they are not yet asking, we want you to be proactive and show them anyway. Or you can wait around until they do, then scramble for the answers (not recommended!). Whenever I (Don) get together with trainers, I ask, "How much pressure are you getting from top management to prove the value of your training programs in results, such as dollars and cents?" More and more often, trainers say that they are feeling such pressure.

OK, let us roll up our sleeves and get into level 4. An important point that establishes the foundation for level 4 is that it is important to *start with the end in mind*. Let your stakeholders define for you *their expectations* for your program. Once you are in clear agreement with them about that, it is then time to go about the business of identifying specific metrics that will best demonstrate and deliver on those expectations. Ultimately, we are tasked with delivering on stakeholder expectations, which leads us to the term we think best describes the Kirkpatrick evaluation model—"return on expectations."

When we look at the objectives of training programs, or talk with stakeholders, we find that almost all aim at accomplishing some worthy result. Often, it is improved quality, improved customer satisfaction, increased productivity, or fewer accidents. In other programs, the objective is improved employee engagement, faster turnaround times, cost savings, larger market share, or increased share of wallet. These and similar expectations can be easily converted to desired level 4 metrics.

Here is how the interplay of curriculum and evaluation works. In planning training programs, trainers need to look at the desired end results and say to themselves and others, "What behavior on the part of supervisors and managers will achieve these results?" Then they determine, "What knowledge, skills, and attitudes do supervisors need in order to behave in that way?" Finally, they determine the curriculum that will meet the training needs, and proceed to do the things described in Chapter 1. In so doing, they hope (and sometimes pray) that the trainees will like the program; learn the knowledge, skills, and attitudes taught; and transfer them to the job. The first three levels of evaluation attempt to determine the degree to which these three things have been accomplished. With these matters determined, methods and tools for evaluation can be decided on. Herein lies the secret to level 4: As mentioned at the end of Chapter 5, if you do a good job with levels 1, 2, and 3, level 4 generally takes care of itself.

The world of professional sports seems to understand this concept much better than the world of work does. Let's look at a specific sports example that illustrates this point. The year this book was written, 2007, the Indianapolis Colts won the Superbowl of American football. Their head coach is Tony Dungy, who understands how to achieve a successful level 4 as well as anyone, and knows that level 3 in particular is the key. In a book called *God Is My CEO*, Dungy's story is told in a chapter called "Tony Dungy: Pressure from the Outside: Sticking to God's Plan Produces Results." Here is Tony's view of winning at football, and our view of winning in business:

> I define success as 'doing the very best you are capable of doing' [level 3]. Of course, it's good when that [level 3] translates into wins, playoffs, and a Superbowl [level 4], but no such outcome is guaranteed. If all we

think about are Superbowls and winning [level 4], then we will compromise and take our focus off being the best we can be [level 3]. I talk to every player on the team. . . . 'You guys that handle responsibility [level 3] will be successful [level 4]. The more we accept personal responsibility and help each other [level 3], the quicker we will achieve our success' [level 4].

Though these were just words at the time he penned them, they *did* come true as his team became world champions. What he is saying, and has actually said to Jim in no uncertain terms, is that if you take care of executing the right behaviors, the results tend to take care of themselves. So it is in our world, but we don't comprehend it the way professional and amateur sports teams and individual athletes do.

Here are some guidelines that will be helpful in tackling level 4.

## Guidelines for Evaluating Results

1. Use a control group if practical.
2. Allow time for results to be achieved.
3. Measure both before and after the program if practical.
4. Repeat the measurement at appropriate times.
5. Keep in mind you are charged with demonstrating Return on Expectations (ROE).
6. Be satisfied with evidence if proof is not possible.

While these guidelines are similar to those of the other levels, they vary in the degree to which they are achievable. Number 3, for instance, is much easier to accomplish at level 4 than at any of the other levels.

## Use a Control Group if Practical

The reason for control groups is always the same: to eliminate the factors other than training that could have caused the changes observed to take place. In a sales training program, for example, it might be quite easy to use control groups. If salespeople in different parts of the country are selling the same products, then a new sales training program can be conducted in some areas and not in others. By measuring the sales figures at various times after the program and comparing them with sales before the program, you can readily see differences. The change in sales in the regions where the new sales program has been presented can easily be compared to the change in areas where the program has not been presented. This does not prove conclusively that the difference resulted from the training program, even if the control and experimental groups were similar. Other factors may have influenced the sales and may include new competitors, the loss of a vital customer, a change in the local economy, or an unusually high employee turnover. We believe, however, that even if you cannot *prove* that training significantly impacted one area over the other, you can get good information that will help you make decisions to either go forward or not with bringing the training to the rest of the enterprise.

## Allow Time for Results to Be Achieved

Executives get a bit impatient about results. The whole "flavor of the month" mentality promotes the expectation of immediate results, or "Let's move on to something else since this obviously is not working." One of the biggest challenges learning professionals face is the pressure for immediate results. It is important that for mission-critical programs, you do whatever you can to educate managers at all levels that (1) it takes time for the reinforcement of learning to create new on-the-job habits, and (2) it takes a while longer for outcomes (results) to show up in full force—sometimes as long as a year. Therefore, in the sales example just cited, time has to elapse before you want to take a good look at the outcomes and announce, "Look what effect training has had!" Specifically, we have to wonder, "How long does it take for a customer to increase orders?" There is no sure answer to the question because each situation is different. Likewise, if a program aims to implement a new style of leadership, the time between training and application on the job may be different for each individual. In deciding on the time lapse before evaluating, a trainer must consider all the factors that are involved. It is important, however, in mission-critical training programs to keep conducting level 3 evaluations, as this will provide you with leading indicators that will tell you whether the expected results will be forthcoming or not.

## Measure Both Before and After the Program if Practical

This one should be a no-brainer. As we mentioned above, it is relatively easy to gather level 4 data and information before and after a program, since it is typically available as business metrics or human resource metrics (e.g., turnover and promotion rates). If, for instance, a program is aimed at reducing the frequency and severity of accidents, figures are readily available. Figures are also available for the sales example just used. The same is true for quality, production, turnover, number of grievances, and absenteeism. For morale and attitudes, preprogram figures may also be available from attitude surveys and performance appraisal forms. This is why we said earlier that gathering level 4 data is not hard—they have been colleted long before your program was ever in existence. The challenge is to link those results with training.

## Repeat the Measurement at Appropriate Times

Each organization must decide how often and when to evaluate. Results can change at any time in either a positive or negative direction. It is up to the training professional to determine the influence of training on these results. For example, sales may have increased because of a big push and close supervision to use a new technique. When the push is over and the boss has other things to do, the salesperson may go back to the old way, and negative results may occur. While scorecards and dashboards are a great way to demonstrate level 4 data at a given time, it is important to collect data and information on an ongoing basis if you want to ensure that you are maximizing the benefits of your training programs.

## Return on Expectations (ROE)

Level 4 metrics should come from your stakeholders. This is often easier said than done. Jim worked with a company a while back that stated their strategy for the next year was to "complete our drive to excellence." When he attempted to find out what senior executives meant by that, he got vague and inconsistent responses. That, in turn, made it difficult to develop targeted training and evaluation since they could not start with the end in mind, since the "end" was not defined clearly enough to be measurable. It is not unusual for training professionals, in their role as internal business partners, to have to poke and prod and even suggest to stakeholders what these expected and/or desired outcomes might look like. We encourage them to always ask the question "What would success look like for you?" Answers to this and related questions can usually be worked with enough to get clarity to identify useful level 4 metrics.

How much does it cost to evaluate at this level and obtain a positive return on expectations? Generally, it is not nearly as costly as it is to evaluate change in behavior. As we said before, since figures you need are usually available, the difficulty is to determine just which ones are the most meaningful, and to what extent they are related, directly or otherwise, to the training.

The amount of money that should be spent on level 4 evaluation should be determined by the amount of money that the training program costs, the potential results that can accrue because of the program, and the number of times that the program will be offered. The higher the value of potential results and the more times the program will be offered, the more time and money should be spent. Once snags have been cleared and accurate numbers start coming in, it is then relatively easy to develop a chain of evidence that will demonstrate a significant contribution in relation to stakeholder expectations.

## Be Satisfied with Evidence if Proof Is Not Possible

The Kirkpatrick model leans heavily on the word "evidence," as we believe that it is rare that you can limit factors enough to create true proof. How much evidence does your top management expect from you? It is important to find out before you go ahead with an evaluation plan. Specifically, find out about what type of evidence will be most compelling to them, and in what form. Then, develop your evaluation plan in such a way as to gather evidence that they will find meaningful. And, again, let us emphasize that compelling evidence usually "wins the day" with executives, especially if you use a balance of data to win their minds, and information to win their hearts.

In a program I (Don) evaluated at the Management Institute of the University of Wisconsin, we conducted patterned interviews after three months with the participants as well as with their supervisors. Among other questions, we asked both of them for changes in behavior as well as results. Tables 6.1 and 6.2 show the results of those evaluations. The figures are in percentages: The first figure is what the participants answered, and the second figure is what their bosses said. At any rate, the results of the evaluations do provide a good deal of evidence that the training made a significant contribution to expected results.

## Collecting Level 4 Data and Information

Level 4 data can be obtained by two major methods—borrowing it from your internal partners, or gathering it yourself. Before asking to borrow data, it is important to know what data would be important to have. As mentioned above, this is best determined prior to a program even being developed. It should be part of the assessment process. A sales manager for a company I (Don) worked with asked that a training program be developed to help his sales associates make better presentations to prospective clients. Instead of encouraging him to rush out and put a program together, there were some tactful questions I asked him first.

> "What do you see that leads you to believe a program on presenting skills would be helpful?"
> "What kinds of things have you tried already?"
> "Have they previously been exposed to presentation techniques in some other training?" (Note that I was trying to find out if they had the skills, but not the follow-up to complete the transfer of learning to on-the-job behavior.)

I asked some other related questions to find out the actual need for the class, and once I was convinced that a program on presenting skills was indicated, I asked, "What kind of results are you hoping to see come from this training?" Well, the sales manager was a bit vague at first, but with some encouraging and prompting, he came up with the following:

Table 6.1. Change in Behavior

| Supervisory areas | Much better | Somewhat better | No change | Somewhat worse | Much worse | Don't know |
|---|---|---|---|---|---|---|
| Giving orders | 25, 12 | 70, 65 | 5, 14 | 0, 0 | 0, 0 | 0, 9 |
| Training | 22, 17 | 56, 39 | 22, 39 | 0, 0 | 0, 0 | 0, 5 |
| Making decisions | 35, 14 | 58, 58 | 7, 23 | 0, 0 | 0, 0 | 0, 5 |
| Initiating change | 21, 9 | 53, 53 | 26, 30 | 0, 0 | 0, 0 | 0, 7 |
| Appraising employee performance | 21, 7 | 50, 42 | 28, 36 | 0, 0 | 0, 0 | 0, 12 |
| Preventing and handling grievances | 12, 7 | 42, 40 | 46, 46 | 0, 0 | 0, 0 | 0, 7 |
| Attitude toward job | 37, 23 | 37, 53 | 26, 23 | 0, 0 | 0, 0 | 0, 0 |
| Attitude toward subordinates | 40, 7 | 42, 60 | 19, 30 | 0, 0 | 0, 0 | 0, 2 |
| Attitude toward management | 42, 26 | 26, 35 | 32, 37 | 0, 0 | 0, 0 | 0, 2 |

Table 6.2. Results

| Performance benchmarks | Much better | Somewhat better | No change | Somewhat worse | Much worse | Don't know |
|---|---|---|---|---|---|---|
| Quantity of production | 5, 5 | 43, 38 | 50, 50 | 0, 2 | 0, 0 | 0, 5 |
| Quality of production | 10, 7 | 60, 38 | 28, 52 | 0, 0 | 0, 0 | 0, 2 |
| Safety | 21, 7 | 28, 37 | 49, 56 | 0, 0 | 0, 0 | 0, 0 |
| Housekeeping | 23, 14 | 32, 35 | 42, 46 | 0, 5 | 0, 0 | 0, 0 |
| Employee attitudes and morale | 12, 7 | 56, 53 | 28, 32 | 2, 5 | 0, 0 | 0, 2 |
| Employee attendance | 7, 2 | 23, 19 | 67, 77 | 0, 0 | 0, 0 | 0, 0 |
| Employee promptness | 7, 2 | 32, 16 | 58, 81 | 0, 0 | 0, 0 | 0, 0 |
| Employee turnover | 5, 0 | 14, 16 | 79, 79 | 0, 5 | 0, 0 | 0, 0 |

1. I would like to see my sales team increase annual sales by 20 percent.
2. I would like to see my sales team improve customer retention by 40 percent.
3. I would like to see more enthusiasm from my sales associates for our products.
4. I would like to see 25 percent less turnover from my sales associates.

Guess what we decided to use for level 4 metrics? Annual sales, customer retention, and staff turnover (we decided to include "enthusiasm" under level 2 attitudes). Are those numbers going to be hard to collect? No! They are numbers that are readily available, and have been for a long time. We typically borrow data from two sources—the business unit itself (e.g., annual sales and customer retention) and Human Resources (e.g., employee turnover). The good news with these metrics is that we have a "before" and "after" for the program we develop. This will allow for some valuable analyses and reporting.

Now, in the example above, an obvious yet important question comes up: "Is it reasonable to expect that one course or program on Effective Sales Presentations will lead to all those desired results?" The answer is probably "no," but a well-planned course with good follow-up can certainly have a strong *influence* on those numbers, which can be counted as "evidence."

Let us now look to the best practices of companies that have been good enough to provide us with case studies over the past years and see what kind of metrics they have borrowed from business and human resources partners.

In evaluating a leadership program, the Gap Inc. borrowed the following metrics from the lines of business and human resources to evaluate their training effectiveness:

*Sales*: It was assumed that if the leadership skills of store managers improved (level 3), employee performance would improve, customers would be served better, and sales would increase.

*Employee turnover*: Studies indicate that recruitment, hiring, and on-the-job training costs are about 1.5 times the first-year salary for a job. Therefore, any training interventions that reduced turnover contribute directly to the bottom line.

*Shrinkage*: It was also assumed that by improving store manager effectiveness, shrinkage as a percentage of sales should go down.

Caterpillar, Inc. identified the following level 4 metrics that they would use for their leadership development programs: productivity, employee engagement, and product quality.

The Canada Revenue Agency developed a fine three-day training program to orient and train newly promoted frontline supervisors. They decided to use morale, teamwork, turnover, and production as metrics that would best demonstrate success of their program.

Gruba Iberdrola is an energy giant in Western Europe. They, too, saw fit to identify and borrow business metrics to show the ultimate effects of a coaching and counseling program for managers. They write, "The level 4 criteria that were selected were those that corresponded to the strategic goals of the departments that were most influenced by the tasks related to the content of the course." We cannot think of a better definition of Kirkpatrick level 4 than that. Specific metrics that they decided on included workload distribution, key performance indicators, meeting deadlines, commercial activity, and profits.

Finally, Cisco Systems, Inc. reports in their case study that "the first step was to identify the desired business results. From this basis, the training program was planned and implemented [and evaluated]." Their training included such borrowed metrics as the reduction in the dollar amount of write-off for untraceable RTVs (Return to Vendor work), decrease in queue and reduced aging of RTVs in the system, reduction in the dollar value of RTV inventory, and immediate increase in productivity.

The second way to gather level 4 data and information is to get it yourself. While this takes quite a bit more effort than borrowing it, oftentimes the data you need are not readily available and additional effort from learning people is required to acquire it. This, however, can be easier than it sounds. We suggest you use the same methods as described in the previous chapter—level 3—and just tag on questions that will provide you with the level 4 data and

Exhibit 6.1. Quick Wins Score Sheet

---

Name: _____

Please respond to the following questions in preparation for the one-day Leadership Development follow-up session. In addition to helping you prepare for this session, your responses will help us to better understand how you have applied what you have learned. This information will help us to learn from the pilot experience and ultimately improve the full deployment of the Leadership Development initiative.

1. What are you doing differently as a result of what you have learned from Leadership Development?

   _____

   _____

   _____

   _____

   _____

   _____

2. Have these actions improved:

   a. Your effectiveness as a leader?        Yes_____  No_____  Not sure _____

   b. Your team's effectiveness?             Yes_____  No_____  Not sure _____

   c. Your organization's performance?       Yes_____  No_____  Not sure _____

3. If you feel that your actions have improved effectiveness, please indicate in what areas:

      i. Productivity                    _____

     ii. Employee engagement            _____

    iii. Quality of work                _____

    iv. Decision-making                  _____

      v. Clarity about priorities        _____

    vi. Communications                  _____

   vii. Collaboration                   _____

   viii. Time to complete projects        _____

    ix. Other: _____     _____
           _____

4. What other benefits have you, your team, and/or the organization realized so far from Leadership Development?

   _____

   _____

Exhibit 6.1. Quick Wins Score Sheet (*continued*)

---

---

---

---

Thank you!

---

information you require. For instance, include in a survey questions about outcomes, or add a couple of questions about results in focus groups.

Our colleagues at Caterpillar provide us with a good example of a questionnaire that combines a bit of level 3 with level 4. (See Exhibit 6.1.)

---

# Caterpillar, Inc.

## Caterpillar University
### Merrill C. Anderson, Ph.D., CEO MetrixGlobal, LLC
### Chris Arvin, Dean, Leadership Development
### Peoria, Illinois

We are now going to share an underutilized yet often wildly effective method of obtaining significant level 4 data. After a program, say on sales training, has had a chance to be reinforced through coaching and level 3 evaluation, and results have had a chance to follow, simply send an e-mail to the managers of the various sales departments that were represented in the training. Along with a warm welcome and a reminder of the sales training that was delivered, ask two questions:

1. Have you noticed any change in the volume of sales during the past six months (be sure to coincide that number with the training)? If so, please provide specifics.
2. To what degree do you attribute the change to the sales training that your people went through? What makes you

think the sales training had something to do with it (please provide evidence)?

Positive answers to those questions can go a long way toward providing evidence—from your key stakeholders!!—that the training has made a significant impact.

## Intangible Benefits

We are big believers in including intangible benefits in any comprehensive package that attempts to provide level 4 evidence for the value of a course or program. Looking to Caterpillar once again, intangible benefits that resulted from their major leadership training program were as follows:

1. Improved strategic focus in decision-making, enabling leaders to focus on the most strategically critical decisions, and not just those decisions that were the most urgent and not necessarily the most strategic.
2. Improved performance management of subordinate leaders, as clearer expectations for performance were set and more effective leadership styles were adopted.
3. Increased accountability for results, as leaders became more involved in setting performance targets and their personal roles in achieving these targets were given greater visibility.
4. Increased insights into personal development needs, as leaders better grasped how their actions impacted the climate of the organization and the performance of their teams and managers.
5. Higher employee engagement, as organizational climate improved and people were able to make a stronger link from their behavior to achieving the organizational goals. People felt more empowered to act without necessarily having to go through a series of approved steps. Teamwork improved and communications became more effective and focused.

## Summary

Evaluating Results, level 4, provides an interesting challenge to training professionals. After all, that is why we train, and we ought to be able to show tangible results that more than pay for the cost of the training. In some cases, such evaluation can be done quite easily. Programs that aim at increasing sales, reducing accidents, reducing turnover, and reducing scrap rates can often be evaluated in terms of tangible results. We, however, stop short of trying to *isolate* those effects, as we have a strong belief in the business partnership model, which includes and encourages additional learning factors such as self-learning, coaching, follow-up, external incentives, refresher training, and mission-critical behavioral reinforcement (largely through level 3).

We believe in finding out what success will look like in the eyes of our stakeholders—internal business leaders—and then working our programs so that they impact those specific expectations and subsequent (level 4) metrics. We then work to gather evidence for a trail that leads from our training efforts to desired outcomes.

It is obviously important to know what your executives expect. If they are satisfied by what they have heard from the participants and their bosses, be thankful. But look ahead and expect them to be looking for more tangible evidence in the future. If you have executives who want tangible evidence, we hope this book gives you some practical ideas on how to provide it.

The most frequent question we are asked is "How do you evaluate level 4?" If you ask us this question, be prepared for our answer.

We will probably describe at length all four levels, beginning with level 1. And the next chapter will tell you why.

# Chapter 7

# Building a Chain of Evidence

Jim was talking with Linda, a learning professional from a large company in Minneapolis, not long ago. She was visibly upset as she related the story of sitting in a sales business meeting with a colleague. First of all, they were "squeezed into" the corner of the table (at least they had a proverbial seat at the table), and they sat quietly while the senior sales manager went through the sales numbers from the past quarter. He was rather proud of the numbers, and even more proud of himself, and how he had led "his" team to feats of great sales success. Linda turned to her learning colleague and whispered, "Some of that is ours!!" Many of you are smiling, as you understand exactly what she was saying. She was pointing out that (1) learning had made a significant contribution to those high sales numbers, and (2) they were not getting any credit.

Well, let us see if we can help Linda and others of you in the same boat. Much of what we have talked about up to this point is vital if one is interested in determining whether to continue a program or not, or to improve one. The evaluation data and information collected at each of the four levels are designed to *loop back* to make those decisions. The purpose of this chapter is to emphasize the importance of evaluating the four levels, or as many as you can, in sequence. This is to be done in a *linear fashion* to be able to *build a compelling chain of evidence as to the value of learning to the bottom line.* This value must be presented in such a way as to *maximize the meaningfulness* to the hearts and minds of your internal stakeholders. The term "chain" is critical, as each level "links" to the next. Only then can you expect increased training budgets and a sense of commitment from them to carry out needed changes that evaluation data suggest must be made in order to achieve organizational directives.

Each level is related to the next one, and none should be skipped. I (Don) recently got a call from a colleague at Microsoft who asked, "Don, we have evaluated our program at levels 1 and 2. Is it OK to skip level 3 and go directly to level 4?"

My answer was "*No!*"

I have often been asked if it is OK to evaluate return on investment without going through the four levels, and again my answer was "no."

Let us build a metaphor here that will help explain how building a chain of evidence to convince executives and line-of-business leaders that training is an important contributor to the bottom line of the business. Many companies that we work with do an excellent job of improving courses and programs. Others are extremely effective at using level 3 to reinforce behaviors on the job. But, there are not many that are really good at convincing senior executives that training is more than just a cost center.

Several years ago, there was a famous person in the United States who was accused of taking advantage of inside information in stock deals. She became rich (richer) as a result of her actions, but also ended up in prison. The headlines announcing her conviction stated, "Trail of Evidence Convicts Martha Stewart." Apparently there was no single piece of evidence that convinced the jury of her guilt. The attorneys for the prosecution spent months talking with witnesses, reviewing documents, and studying points of the laws in order to pull together enough different types of evidence to bring about the conviction. What we have done was to change the word "trail" to "chain."

Now, let us tie this to evaluation. *You* are the attorney. It is your job to gather evidence to convince the jury—in this case, all of your key business stakeholders—of the value of training as a competitive variable for the business' bottom line. This is what I (Don) meant in my original writings when I said that one of the purposes of evaluation is to "justify the (trainers') existence." Also in keeping with my past writings is the notion that we are looking for *evidence*, not proof. Despite years of claims and articles on cost-benefit calculations, we still believe it is not possible to *prove* that a particular training event led to a specific bottom-line contribution. So, we focus on the true training-business partnership model of generating a carefully crafted package of objective data and subjective information—from level 1 through level 4—to provide the evidence of the value of training. This sharply contrasts with the notion of overreliance on one piece of "proof " (a cost-benefit percentage determined by "isolating" the effects of training).

Let us jump to a real case example, then get back to the metaphor. A major hospitality company that we worked with recently went before their Board of Directors to demonstrate to them the value of their Corporate University. They had lots of level 1 data pointing out that the career development and leadership programs were extremely well received. They also had lots of pre– and post–level 2 data that provided a good deal of evidence that learning was achieved during the programs. They also borrowed data from Human Resources that showed that those who participated in career development programs were significantly more likely to receive internal promotions. They also had colorful graphs and charts to illustrate these data. After the Corporate University team gave their presentation, the president of the company said, "This is all very impressive. I do have a couple of questions—what specific behaviors did your Career Development program participants engage in that made the biggest impact on their promotions? And, what specific behaviors did the supervisors of the participants do that leveraged success of their direct reports? After all, we want to be clear about those behaviors so we can focus on them in future training and coaching." After an uncomfortable pause, the dean of the Corporate University responded, "We don't know, but we will find out!" She then set out to develop a robust level 3 evaluation methodology that did indeed answer those questions. If the boardroom had been a courtroom, and the board members, members of the jury, then they might have had to say, "We find for the defendant."

As the "primary lawyer," it is your job to gather this evidence. You must also determine what type of evidence will be the most compelling to your audience. Jim tells the true story of trying to convince the board of directors of a major midwestern bank of the value of a particular "soft-skills" training program. At first, Jim presented data from each of the four levels in sequence. He presented data that showed high customer satisfaction (level 1), a positive change in attitude toward job and company (level 2), new on-the-job behaviors that supported the new corporate strategy (level 3), and some preliminary positive external customer satisfaction scores (level 4). The graphs and charts and PowerPoint slides were works of art. But it was not until he brought a personal testimonial of one of the participants to the court-room (I mean, boardroom), who gushed over the "personal and pro-fessional care and interest displayed by the company," that the board deemed the effort valuable.

Let us dig into the details of this critical concept. Our chain of evi-dence in evaluation begins with level 1, the Reaction from the trainees. Some trainers call Reaction sheets "happiness ratings" or "smile sheets," and that is exactly what they are. But they do it in a way that indicates they do not believe they are important.

There are four reasons why level 1 is important:

- By asking trainees to complete a Reaction sheet, you are telling them that their input is important. If you do not ask them to complete the form, you are telling them that their reaction is not important and that trainers know best.
- The reactions must be measured so that you know how well the program is being received. If they are unhappy with the program, their attitudes toward the program and the trainers can cause them to have a lack of interest in the program and they will get very little benefit from it. If the reactions are pos-itive, their interest and attitude remain high and the chances of learning are great.
- Trainees will be asked by their bosses and others, "How was the training program you attended?" There is a very good chance that their answers will get to higher-level manage-ment. If the reactions are positive, higher-level managers will feel good about the program, and in some cases they need no further evidence because their philosophy is that "our people are our most important asset, and what they say is good enough for me." If they hear negative comments, they may presume that the program is not effective, even though they have no tangible evidence, and they certainly do not do a survey to see whether or not the comments they have heard are common. Remember, the trainees are your customers and customer sat-isfaction is very important.
- Getting an indication of how satisfied the trainees are with the program, and to what degree they find it relevant to

their job, is critical to setting the stage for actual learning (level 2), on-the-job application (level 3), and ultimate results (level 4).

In summary, satisfaction with the training and program relevance to the job are two important level 1 ingredients that comprise the beginning of this chain of evidence.

The chain of evidence continues with level 2, Learning. This is essential in determining the effectiveness of a training program. It is useless to evaluate Behavior or Results without first evaluating Learning.

Hopefully, the training program is based on the needs of the trainees. What knowledge, skills, and attitudes do they need to do their job effectively? In one of the training programs at Intel, the evaluators found that the knowledge and skills they were teaching did not transfer to the job because they were not related to the job! What a waste, and how much frustration for all concerned. The trainers were trying to teach knowledge and skills the learners could not apply. And how frustrating for trainees to sit through a program where they were "learning" things they could not apply. And how frustrating it is for the managers of the trainees to discover that the program was a waste of time.

The chain of evidence picks up here from level 1 in that in order to demonstrate the value of a program, you must be able to show that the trainees came away with targeted new learning in the form of knowledge, skills, and/or changed attitudes. If you are trying to build this chain, you will generally need to show what kind of change has occurred specifically because of and during the program, thus necessitating some type of pre- and postassessment. Knowledge tests and checks, skills observations, surveys, and questionnaires can all fit this need.

The next step in the evaluation of the chain of evidence is measuring level 3, Behavior. It does no good to try to convince a group of business leaders or other stakeholders of the value of your training efforts if you cannot show them how learning and good coaching led to behavior change on the job. And here is where Chapter 2 becomes important—how effective are trainers in getting support from line managers? We were asked in a session a short time ago, "If you can demonstrate learning and ultimately the results you were seeking were realized, why do you need to show level 3?" The answer is this:

The results could have come from a variety of factors, and if you do not know how well learning transferred to on-the-job behavior, you will not be able to take any credit for the success.

The final step in this chain is level 4, Results. Read this paragraph carefully, as it is a good summary of how this whole four-level chain of evidence works. *If* you have done a good job of ensuring that the training atmosphere was conducive to learning (and you have evidence to show that), and you can document that targeted learning actually took place, which then led to mission-critical on-the-job behaviors, *then* the level 4 results that were identified in the assessment phase of the development of the program should bear out this fantastic and compelling relationship between learning and business outcomes.

Below is a final report from a colleague of ours, Jim Hashman from Comcast Cable, Inc. This fine report demonstrates that Jim and Comcast Cable fully understand the power of the four levels to develop a compelling chain of evidence that clearly shows, "Hey, our training really made a contribution to the bottom line. Hurray!!"

---

## Comcast St. Paul 2006 PRIDE Call Flow Coaching Program Overview

### Jim Hashman
### Midwest Division Director
### Sales Learning and Development
### Comcast University

Comcast University is the progressive learning and development organization within Comcast Corporation, the nation's leader in cable television, high-speed Internet, and consumer phone services. The university, led by Chief Learning Officer Martha Soehren, partners with Comcast field operations units to create and implement knowledge, skill, and leadership development solutions addressing existing and future business requirements.

During the spring of 2006, the St. Paul call center senior management team requested support from Comcast University to help create a sales improvement program for its nearly 300 inbound customer service and sales representatives known as Customer Account Executives (CAEs). This task was the responsibility of Jim Hashman, the Midwest Division Director of Sales Learning and Development.

Implementing the ADDIE model (Analyze, Design, Develop, Implement, and Evaluate), Jim began by conducting a thorough needs assessment beginning with the end in mind. Jim initially focused his analysis conversations on level 4 by drilling down on the key performance indicators and existing business metrics the call center used to evaluate performance in the marketplace. Once the metrics for success were determined, the questioning moved to level 3 by asking, "What observable behaviors result in the targeted business metric?" Upon identifying the observable behaviors, each behavior was defined in terms of requisite skills and knowledge (level 2). Finally, the university was prepared to implement their standard level 1 questionnaire during implementation. Using this level 4–3–2–1 analysis approach, the university team was then prepared to show a chain of evidence with solid links from level 1 through level 4 during their postimplementation evaluation phase.

Continuing with the ADDIE model, the program's design included four objectives:

- Improve the customer's experience.
- Increase CAE core selling skills.
- Provide frontline supervisors with coaching tools to improve the customer's experience and develop CAE core selling skills.
- Have fun in the classroom and on the job while learning new skills.

The development phase maintained an emphasis on evaluation by incorporating several level 2 activities into the classroom experience. These activities required learners to demonstrate their understanding of key concepts and skills in a variety of group and individual exercises, including

- identifying skill usage in recorded examples.
- teach-back opportunities.
- role-play modeling and feedback.

The implementation leveraged a train-the-trainer format, with the frontline supervisors conducting the actual training for their respective teams. These sessions were organized into six sequential segments conducted every other week over a twelve-week period. Level 3 evaluation began early in the implementation as mystery shoppers called to evaluate the actual on-the-job performance of the CAEs. These calls provided additional feedback opportunities for learners as well as quantified individual and team performance. The data were used to make real-time, mid-implementation adjustments to curriculum, feedback, and follow-up.

Although evaluation activities were continuous throughout the analysis, design, development, and implementation phases, Comcast University continued to partner with the call center operations to follow the chain of evidence from the classroom to the marketplace. Their level 1 through level 4 results follow.

## Level 1

The level 1 surveys revealed:

- 95 percent of respondents ($n=551$) agreed that terms and issues were communicated clearly.
- 94.8 percent of respondents ($n=564$) will be able to incorporate the course into the activities of their team, unit, or department.
- 95.7 percent of respondents ($n=566$) will use the skills in their daily activities.
- 87 percent of respondents ($n=564$) would recommend the course.
- 94.1 percent of respondents ($n=550$) agree that the exercises were relevant to their job.

Considering that these results were from training conducted by supervisors rather than professional trainers, Comcast believes the program was a great success from both the learners' perspectives and the design and development perspective.

## Level 2

Comcast University favors non-test-centric level 2 methodologies (for noncertification training) such as teach backs, role-play exercises, and review discussions. Each of these techniques was incorporated throughout the twelve-week program. Given that 95 percent of participants felt the terms and issues were communicated clearly, Comcast is confident that the program successfully facilitated skill and knowledge transfer.

## Level 3

Following the chain of evidence out of the classroom and into the workplace, Comcast contracted CSR, Inc., of Wayne, Pennsylvania, to place six mystery shopper calls per CAE into the St. Paul call center over the twelve-week implementation period. The mystery callers were trained in the program's skills and expectations prior to making their calls. Once connected to a CAE, the mystery caller pretended to be a current or potential customer while evaluating the CAE's skill usage. At the completion of the call, the mystery caller gave the CAE positive feedback on his or her skill usage and made any applicable suggestions for improvement. In an effort to make the learning and performance fun, an incentive was created to reward skills demonstrated on the random mystery calls.

The data provided by CSR, Inc. demonstrated the following:

- 8 of 10 overall telephone skills improved over the pretraining baseline.
- The incidence of skill mastery for all skills increased 43 percent.
- 5 of 5 core sales skills improved over the pretraining baseline.
- The incidence of sales skills mastery increased 78 percent.

The final piece of Comcast University's level 3 analysis was their customer satisfaction survey. Comcast routinely surveys customers who have recently called into their call centers. One of the key CAE-specific survey items, and a clear component of the training, was the CAE's ability to treat the caller as a valued customer. Adding to the chain of evidence, the St. Paul call center realized an immediate improvement in the percentage of customers who felt the CAE treated them as a valued customer.

## Level 4

Completing their evaluation, Comcast University followed the chain of evidence into the marketplace by using the Key Performance

Indicators (KPIs) discussed in the analysis stage of the project. The predetermined KPIs indicated a pre- and posttraining improvement of

- 11 percent in the video sales–related metric.
- 22 percent in the revenue-related metric.
- 28 percent in the Internet sales–related metric.
- 62 percent in the transitional sales–related metric.

Since an effective chain of evidence is typically composed of a blend of data (objective) and information (subjective), following are comments made by participants that demonstrate "value from the eye of the beholders."

### CAE Feedback

- It lets you be a person.
- It relaxes the customer.
- It disarms the customer when they have their guard up.
- The *Competitive Review* "is awesome."
  ◦ Lets you compare
  ◦ Lets the customer learn who is best
  ◦ Lets you be honest

### Supervisor Feedback

- You can hear the relaxed relationships.
- Coaching sessions that used to take an hour now take 10–15 minutes.

Comcast University's efforts in linking the ADDIE instructional design model and the Kirkpatrick evaluation model aided in their ability to follow the chain of evidence from the classroom to the workplace and from the workplace to the marketplace. By predetermining the business success factors, they were able to objectively identify supporting workplace behaviors. Once the targeted workplace behaviors were agreed upon, they partnered with internal clients to define the requisite skills and knowledge. Evaluating the learner's reaction is a standard operating procedure for Comcast University.

Creating a positive learning environment is a cornerstone of Comcast University's design and facilitation strategies. Driving results is their objective. Following the chain of evidence from the classroom, to the workplace, and out into the marketplace is how they create value.

## Summary

You are the "learning attorneys" who are tasked with demonstrating the value of your learning programs to the bottom line. Gathering evidence that will be meaningful and compelling to your "jury"— your business stakeholders—is critical to the future of your learning function, and perhaps your job! The concept of a chain of evidence simply means that you evaluate each of the four levels, gather the information and data, put them in a compelling final report format, and effectively present the report to your stakeholders. The good news, as we said before, is that if you do a good job by providing compelling evidence at the first three levels, level 4 generally takes care of itself.

# References

## Books

Horton, William. *Evaluating E-Learning*. Alexandria, VA: American Society for Training and Development, 2001.

Kirkpatrick, Donald L. *How to Conduct Productive Meetings*. Alexandria, VA: American Society for Training and Development, 2006.

Kirkpatrick, Donald L. *Improving Employee Performance through Appraisal and Coaching*. 2nd ed. New York: AMACOM, 2006.

Kirkpatrick, Donald L. *Managing Change Effectively*. Woburn, MA: Butterworth-Heinemann, 2001.

Kirkpatrick, Donald L., and James D. Kirkpatrick. *Evaluating Training Programs: The Four Levels*. 3rd ed. San Francisco, CA: Berrett-Koehler Publishers, 2006.

Kirkpatrick, Donald L., and James D. Kirkpatrick. *Transferring Learning to Behavior*. San Francisco, CA: Berrett-Koehler Publishers, 2005.

Odiorne, George. *The Change Resistors*. New York: Prentice-Hall, 1981.

## Resources

Here are two resources used by organizations with case studies presented in *Evaluating Training Programs: The Four Levels*, from which the examples in this book are quoted.

Knowledge Advisors (Metrics that Matter). 222 S. Riverside, Suite 1700, Chicago, IL 60606. (Used by Defense Acquisition University.)

Questionmark Corporation. 5 Hillandale Avenue, Stamford, CT 06902. (Used by The Regence Group.)

# Index

DONALD L. KIRKPATRICK holds B.A., M.A., and Ph.D. degrees from the University of Wisconsin in Madison. His dissertation was "Evaluating a Human Relations Training Program for Supervisors." At the Management Institute of the University of Wisconsin, he taught managers at all levels the principles and techniques of many subjects, including Coaching, Communication, Managing Time, Managing Change, Team Building, and Leadership.

In industry, he served as Training Director for International Minerals and Chemical Corp. where he developed a Performance Appraisal Program. Later he served as Human Resources Manager of Bendix Products Aerospace Division.

He is a past national president of the American Society for Training and Development (ASTD) from which he received the Gordon Bliss and Lifetime Achievement in Workplace Learning and Performance awards. He is also a member of *Training Magazine*'s Hall Of Fame.

Don is the author of seven management inventories and seven management books including the third edition of *Evaluating Training Programs: The Four Levels*, which has become the basis for evaluation all over the world. This book has been translated into Spanish, Polish, Turkish, and Chinese. His other books include: *Developing Employees Through Appraisal and Coaching*, second edition (2006); *How To Plan and Conduct Productive Meetings* (2006); and *Managing Change Effectively* (2002).

He is a regular speaker at ASTD and IQPC national conferences, at other professional and company conferences, and a frequent speaker at chapters of ASTD.

As a consultant, he has presented programs to many U.S. organizations and those in many foreign countries including Singapore, Korea, Argentina, Brazil, Saudi Arabia, Malaysia, Greece, the Netherlands, Spain, Australia, and India.

He is Board Chairman of South Asian Ministries, an active member of Gideons International, and a Senior Elder at Elmbrook Church in Brookfield, Wisconsin.

Don's hobbies include fishing, tennis, golf, and music—big band, classical and directing church choirs.

He can be contacted at dleekirk1@aol.com.

*To find out more information about the American
Society for Training and Development, contact
Mark at Mmorrow@astd.com.*

JAMES D. KIRKPATRICK has a B.A. and M.A. from the University of Wisconsin, and a Ph.D. in Counseling Psychology from Indiana State University. Jim has held positions as a fisheries biologist, high school teacher, and clinical psychologist before moving into the world of organizational learning and development in the early 1990s. Since then, he has served as a career development consultant, management consultant, MBA program instructor, and as the founder and director of First Indiana Bank's Corporate University. Jim worked as the senior evaluation consultant for Corporate University Enterprises, Inc. until joining SMR USA Consulting Group in early 2007. Since 1995, he has developed and implemented a career development center, worked on senior strategic planning teams, and consulted with organizations all across the world on Evaluation, Team Building, Coaching, and Leadership,

As major areas of expertise, Jim considers implementing the four levels of evaluation, coaching managers to reinforce training, balanced scorecarding, executing strategy, and aligning curricula with strategy. He wrote the book, *Transferring Learning to Behavior* (2005) and co-authored three books with his father, Don. He has made presentations and conducted workshops in four continents in the past five years.

Jim currently resides in a small community outside Indianapolis, Indiana, but by the time you read this, he may be living on a lake in one of the northern U.S. states. He enjoys fishing, running, camping, tennis, music, watching his son CJ play lacrosse, and spending time with family and friends.

Please visit Jim's company's website at www.smr-usa.com, or email Jim at jim.kirkpatrick@smr-usa.com.

# Berrett–Koehler
## Publishers

A community dedicated to creating
a world that works for all

**Visit Our Website: www.bkconnection.com**

Read book excerpts, see author videos and Internet movies, read our authors' blogs, join discussion groups, download book apps, find out about the BK Affiliate Network, browse subject-area libraries of books, get special discounts, and more!

**Subscribe to Our Free E-Newsletter, the *BK Communiqué***

Be the first to hear about new publications, special discount offers, exclusive articles, news about bestsellers, and more! Get on the list for our free e-newsletter by going to **www.bkconnection.com**.

**Get Quantity Discounts**

Berrett-Koehler books are available at quantity discounts for orders of ten or more copies. Please call us toll-free at (800) 929-2929 or email us at **bkp .orders@aidcvt.com**.

**Join the BK Community**

BKcommunity.com is a virtual meeting place where people from around the world can engage with kindred spirits to create a world that works for all. BKcommunity.com members may create their own profiles, blog, start and participate in forums and discussion groups, post photos and videos, answer surveys, announce and register for upcoming events, and chat with others online in real time. Please join the conversation!

# IMPLEMENTING THE FOUR LEVELS